A Welcoming Life

A Welcoming Life

THE M.F.K. FISHER SCRAPBOOK

Compiled and Annotated by Dominique Gioia

COUNTERPOINT

WASHINGTON, D.C.

A note regarding quoted material in this text: Ellipses that M. F. K. Fisher used as punctuation
in her prose are indicated by closed ellipses (followed by a space), thus: *Rex decided he would
be a geologist probably... possibly...* Ellipses that represent editorial elisions in the quoted
material are indicated by open ellipses, thus: *maybe. . . . And the four of us were undoubtedly
among the first beatniks of the Far West — unwittingly, of course.*

LIBRARY OF CONGRESS CATALOGING-IN-PUBLICATION DATA

Fisher, M. F. K. (Mary Frances Kennedy), 1908–1992

A welcoming life: the M. F. K. Fisher scrapbook / compiled and annotated by Dominique Gioia.

Includes bibliographical references and index.

1. Fisher, M. F. K. (Mary Frances Kennedy), 1908–1992—Biography.   2. Authors,
American—20th century—Biography.   3. Food writers—United States—Biography.
4. Fisher, M. F. K. (Mary Frances Kennedy), 1908–1992—Pictorial works.
I. Gioia, Dominique.   II. Title.

PS3511.17428Z4694   1997

641'.092—dc21

[B]   96–54641

ISBN 1-887178-32-5 (alk. paper)

FIRST PRINTING

Designed and electronically produced by David Bullen.

Printed in Canada on acid-free paper that meets the American
National Standards Institute Z39-48 Standard.

COUNTERPOINT

P.O. Box 65793

Washington, D.C. 20035-5793

Distributed by Publishers Group West.

Contents

Introduction

M. F. K. Fisher's life is not easily captured, in pictures or otherwise, for she shunned the categorical, the reductive. Though generally recognized as one of the century's finest American prose stylists, author of more than twenty books, Fisher shied away from even a sense of vocation: "I have known a lot of writers," she wrote, "and have always been basically amused by their frantic insistence on being WRITERS." The Fisher sentence—its artful construction, its elegant juxtapositions, its apparent simplicity—once prompted William Turnbull, a friend and one of Fisher's most stalwart publishers, to suggest that "Great art comes from indirection."

More indirect still than her wonderful, lucent style was Fisher's approach to subject. By writing most particularly about food, she wrote at the same time about life. When recounting the reading of cookbooks, the eating of steak,

the concocting of a cauliflower casserole, she spoke too of comfort and dignity; of the differences between appetites and hungers; of how to be at home when not at home—home being anywhere we are awake to our senses.

But while her books may indirectly throw our lives into high relief, they did not always reveal hers. Here, however, in these personal photographs, Mary Frances is remarkably present. There is a three-quarter profile of her, taken at Le Pâquis in 1938, in which she is seated in a cane-backed chair, looking down at something (or nothing) in her lap and the suggestion of her great capacity for living is as apparent as her radiant, inward happiness. Later pictures, such as one taken with Donald Friede on her thirty-eighth birthday, reveal a guardedness and weary calm, defenses that stanched the rising tide of her life's disorder. A 1954 photograph of Mary Frances on the Cours Mirabeau in

Aix, a daughter at each hand, is poignant evidence of her vulnerability and bravery: she was a single mother introducing her children to life in a foreign country, by choice of course, but alone, without the support of a partner or the security of a plan. Her response to life is there in her face, and these are her private faces. She had a public face, too, but even the stylized glamour of Hollywood publicity portraits don't conceal her confidence, her mettle. (Glamour and thoughtfully measured self-indulgence were themselves, for a time, her response to difficult circumstance.) Many of the photographs in this book's final section have an unmistakable portrait quality as well, though they are no less candidly suffused with the force of Fisher's personality—her intensity and humor both. She was at ease in front of a camera, a natural beauty, and she learned early on to dominate, to play without being coy, seduce without dissembling.

Apart from the psychological insights these pictures offer, it is nothing short of delightful for Fisher's admirers to acquaint themselves with the people and places in her books, to meet Aunt Gwen on Laguna Beach, or Mary Frances, basket in hand, striding through the market in Vevey. All of the images, with a few noted exceptions, come from a large collection of personal and publicity photographs that Fisher assembled throughout her life. A few belongings of importance, first-edition dust jackets from *The Art of Eating* titles among them, were photographed for inclusion. Excerpts from her books, journals, and letters, both published and unpublished, provide a loose narrative link. This is a book of bits and pieces then, a scrapbook, that familiar miscellany by which lives are quilted. Together the scraps add up to an impressionistic yet intensely *seen* biography, one of a woman with the requisite bravery, talent, and steel to engage the good and the bad in life, to exult in and share, through art, the measure of her powers.

D. G.

A Near-Native Californian

1908 — 1928

M. F. K. Fisher preferred to think that she "sprang full-blown at the age of three into a real native life" in California. In fact, she was born Mary Frances Kennedy in Michigan in 1908, the first child of Rex Kennedy, a fourth-generation newspaper man, and "a shy, proud, asocial, snobbish woman," Edith Oliver Holbrook. Another daughter, Anne, was born in 1910, and soon thereafter Rex, Edith, and the two young girls set out for the West Coast. "Rex decided he would be a geologist probably... possibly... maybe. . . . And the four of us were undoubtedly among the first beatniks of the Far West—unwittingly, of course."

The family eventually settled in the predominantly Quaker and not altogether congenial town of Whittier, California, where Rex again fell into newspapering, becoming co-owner and publisher of the Whittier *News*.

More siblings joined the family—Norah was born in 1917 and David two years later—as did Edith's mother, the ascetic Mrs. Holbrook, who came to live with the Kennedys after her husband died. Mrs. Holbrook was a devout Campbellite, exemplary in the strength of her convictions, peremptory in her dismissal of "voluptuary" pleasures. "Grandmother did not believe in any form of seasoning," Mary Frances wrote. "The flatter a thing tasted, the better it was for you. . . . And the better it was for you, she believed, the more you should suffer to eat it, thus proving your innate worth as a Christian, a martyr to the flesh but a courageous one." Grandmother Holbrook and her Nervous Stomach prevailed in the Kennedy household.

An honorary "aunt," Gwen Nettleship Shaw had an equally profound if gentler influence on the Kennedy family. Aunt Gwen was neighbor, companion, and often parental surrogate while Rex ran a newspaper and Edith bore children and convalesced. Mary Frances would one day write about Aunt Gwen: "She flowed through my life, all our lives, like a gusty river bringing food and excitement and adventure. . . . For a long time *we* were the lake into which most of her flowed, from all her generous springs and sources. It was an awesome gift, and we accepted it as our due, much as dry ground accepts fresh water. We *used* her."

A "completely happy person" as a child among family, friends, a well-stocked library, and the California outdoors, Mary Frances would chafe under the pressures of adolescence and the increasing responsibilities of being the oldest child. Rex and Edith decided on boarding school. Drifting uninspired through two such high schools, then "two years of discontented 'college life' in five schools," she was enrolled in a summer program at the University of California at Los Angeles when she met her husband-to-be.

"And as soon as I could escape the trap, whatever it was, I fled family and friends and security like a suddenly freed pigeon, or mole, or wildcat. I probably thought that at last I was MYSELF! And just as probably I would have faltered and even returned with new docility to my cozy cage if I had known how long it would take to start real questioning."

The house in Albion, Michigan, where Mary Frances was born just before midnight on July 3, 1908, "in a supreme effort from my mother, whose husband had assured her that I would be named Independencia if I arrived on the 4th."

Edith Oliver Holbrook Kennedy
with her first child, Mary Frances.

MF, Albion, ca. 1909.

Edith Holbrook and Rex Kennedy the year they were married, 1904. Edith was the youngest of nine children, the daughter of "The Banker" in the small Iowa town where she grew up. MF described her as "a strange combination of prairie princess . . . and a Daisy Miller type. . . . seemingly sophisticated but inwardly naïve." She was educated in boarding schools in America before going to Europe, where her parents sent her with a paid companion, wishfully thinking she'd forget about Rex, "the gawky young journalist she was determined to marry."

Rex Kennedy was drafted into newspapering at a young age by his parents, publishers of weeklies and political broadsides. "Part of his nature was fiery and impatient," MF wrote. "The larger part was timid, at least to the point of believing in predestination as outlined to him by the people he respected and loved, including his wife and her family. He had been meant, *they told him, to be taller, stronger, better equipped to stay respectable and honored, than many people he knew secretly to be much braver and more privileged than himself. His absorbing interest in hungry broken transients was proof positive of this inner doubt and quarrel, I think."*

Albion, August 1910: MF at two, with her sister Anne, four weeks old.

Rex with his two daughters, en route to California, May 1911. "Rex was in love with the idea of a man's leaving his own land and starting a new life in a far country, alone; Edith was resigned to her husband's need for this strange un-Holbrook hunger in him, and protested almost dutifully."

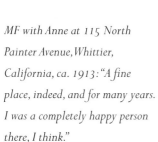

MF with Anne at 115 North Painter Avenue, Whittier, California, ca. 1913: "A fine place, indeed, and for many years. I was a completely happy person there, I think."

Anne and MF with Edith, ca. 1914. "There are almost always several plausible causes for a result such as my early interest in eating and drinking. Perhaps an important one for me was the fact that my little sister Anne had a very finicky digestive system. It made me aware of how one person can eat this but not that, when an-other can eat both... how one person will push a plate away and even then be sick, while another will polish it off and feel rosier than ever. . . .

"[Anne's] emotions and her guts were . . . a capricious team, and as her appointed protector I was strongly aware of that."

The Kennedys with Grandmother Holbrook and an unidentified friend (with hat), ca. 1914. Edith's mother had moved to Whittier to live with the Kennedy family after her husband died. "My father often spoke with gratitude and even affection of her, for without her moral and financial help he might never have weathered the first years there. She was a good solid part of our family life, and Anne and I respected and trusted her, without ever feeling what I think of as love. It was like living within sight of the Rock of Gibraltar. She and her daughter were often chilly, the outward sign of their long hostility, but they never bickered or exchanged ugly words, and Rex presided like a wise Chanticleer over his hennery, smoothing feathers with discretion and occasionally showing his spurs."

MF, ca. 1915. "I still feel embarrassed that I was not born a native Californian because I truly think I am one. I really started to be me somewhere there . . . and I do feel 'native.' So pooh! to all my friends who look at me pityingly when I confess that I was not born in Santa Monica or La Jolla or Montecito."

Edith's mother, Mary Frances Oliver Holbrook. "And if Grandmother had not been the small stout autocrat, forbidding the use of alcohol, spices, fats, tobacco, and the five senses in our household, I might never have discovered that I myself could detail their uses to my own delight.... A Nervous Stomach can be a fine thing in a family tree, in its own way and at least twice removed."

Edith's father, Bernard David Holbrook. "One of the best things about my childhood in Whittier was that several people in the last few generations in the family had been easy marks for book salesmen. Prime culprit was my grandfather Holbrook, ... who died in about 1910 after a long sedentary life of reading, which of course one does not do as well behind a plow, or riding a tiger, as one does in an armchair."

Edith with her father, ca. 1900. "The two refugees from Grandmother's stern Puritanism would read themselves away from the freezing little village on the Midwestern prairies." Throughout her life, Edith stoked her appetite for English novels; she read "whenever she had the faintest excuse not to be doing something else."

Like his son a newspaper man, Rex's father, Clarence Klaude Kennedy, was a born-again Christian and "a giant, very beautiful and subject to violent moods." Late in their lives, he and his wife, Luella, moved to California and farmed a small ranch not far from MF's family in Whittier. "I see him as possessing great strength and dignity that were mine for the taking. I doubt, though, that he felt much more interest in me than I in him. We were as impersonal as two animals of different sex and age but sharing some of the same blood, unaware that we lifted our hooves in a strangely similar way as we headed for the same hay-mangers, the same high hills."

Rex's mother, Luella Green Kennedy, was a college graduate, as was her husband. While raising four sons, she taught Greek and Latin, "and even Anglo-American, in whatever local high school her wandering husband settled near."

Clarence and Luella with Edith, MF, and Anne. Whittier, August 1915. "[Edith] was constitutionally opposed to in-laws, and her whole attitude was that they must perforce be equally antagonistic toward her as the bride who robbed their roost of a fine cock and as a person of a higher social station. . . . It is too bad that my mother waited so long to slough off her conditioned reactions to being related by marriage to people who, in spite of everything she did, were better educated than her own parents but not as affluent. She held us away, willy-nilly, from much warmth, and knowledge, and all that."

The Whittier News staff, 1912. Rex is in the back wearing a dark hat; Harry Holdsworth, co-owner of the paper with Rex, is second from the left in the second row.

Edith, MF, and Anne, ca. 1915.

"As I see it now, our non-Quaker family started out in Whittier with several strikes against us. When I was a child there, though, I was unaware of almost everything except being sturdy and happy. I still have no idea of how much and how often Rex may have been rebuffed and rebuffed as editor of the News, as well as known companion of men who played poker, drank strong liquor, and even went to Mass. As for my mother, she took out whatever social desires she may have had—and they were indeed puny, for by nature and training she was asocial—in working valiantly for the Woman's Club and the small mission which later became the Episcopal church, and in exchanging long cheerful letters with her Eastern relatives... and in running a kind of boardinghouse for anyone even remotely related to her. . . . I think [Rex] knew that his wife's feverish need to open her house to her own clan was a sign that she was, in truth, lonely in her local world of polite but distant Quaker ladies."

Rex, ca. 1915.

Anne and MF in the Maxwell, 1916. "Age is enormous, when anyone is almost without it."

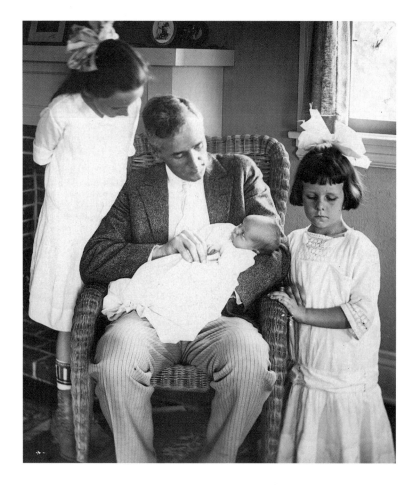

MF and Anne with Rex and three-week-old Norah Kennedy, 1917.

"Related by love alone," Aunt Gwen Shaw with MF, Anne, Norah, and a friend, Laguna Beach. A widow after one night of marriage to an English lieutenant who died while serving in France (he reported for duty the day after their wedding), Gwen had no children of her own. She devoted herself instead to her father and invalid mother, and to the Kennedy family, who lived nearby. "More and more Mother handed over large pieces of her whole matronly existence to the big red-faced Englishwoman, and devoted herself to herself, and of course to the next child. And more

and more Anne and I came to recognize Aunt Gwen as the core of our lives."

Gwen and Rex. "[Gwen] and my father were fine together, in what I think was as near a sexless way as a normally constructed man and woman can be, and I doubt that it was deliberate in its imperson-ality. She was a never-failing companion and help to him, and I think he may have wondered at times, with Professor Higgins, why more women could not be like that."

MF and Anne with Aunt Gwen, Laguna Beach, January 1, 1918. "All I could now say about Aunt Gwen will never be said, but it is sure that much of my enjoyment of the art of living, as well as of eating, comes from her... as well as my certainty that the two are, or can be, synonymous."

MF and Anne, Laguna Beach, ca. 1918.

The cottage at Laguna Beach that Rex built with the help of friends. The Kennedys would go to the beach for weekends in the winter, but in the summer MF and Anne would stay there with Aunt Gwen for weeks or more at a time, hiking, swimming, feasting on Gwen's idiosyncratic specialties like the fried egg sandwiches whose magnificence MF would later ascribe to spiritual as well as physical ingredients. On Sundays Rex and Edith would come out, with or without friends and the two smaller children—"always a pleasurable invasion but basically something to be tolerated until we could be alone again."

Clockwise from left: Gwen's brother Raymond Nettleship, Gwen, Edith, friends Barnie and Peter Maclaren, Virginia and Park Holbrook, Isobel Maclaren, Anne, and MF, ca. 1918.

"Edith was probably at her most open, during those first Laguna years, of all the fifty-some I knew her or was cordially acquainted with her.... I think she was baffled by the cool fact that it mattered less than nothing to the people she was instinctively drawn to in Whittier, the bankers' wives and such, that she had gone to finishing schools and read Goethe and Balzac and lived in Europe: she was simply not a Quaker. She withdrew almost completely from our town as she grew older (which did not make life easier for the rest of us in the family...) In Laguna, though, and for a long time, she was gay, dashing, amusing, the rare bird Rex had caught. I know that she was often harassed, at the beach, by problems like hungry or sick children, tree roots clogging the pipes of stinking water. But spiritually she found her own release in those long-gone Sundays, full of tumult and hard work and communion. And Father did too, in concomitance as well as on his own, and of course conjugally."

Edith and Barnie Maclaren.

June 13, 1920, Anne's tenth birthday party at the ranch, where the family had moved that year. (MF is in the back row, wearing braids and scowling.) The ranch was a small orange grove at the edge of town where it stretched out into countryside. "We had beautiful orchard and citrus fruits, and artichokes, and asparagus and every kind of vegetable that would grow above ground (the soil was impossible for roots like parsnips, thank God...). . . . They all flourished in our Chosen Land, as did the pigeons, chickens, turkeys, pig, cow, Hi-Ho Silver the horse, dogs, cats, children, and other people."

MF and Anne with Grandmother Holbrook and younger siblings David and Norah, 1919. "Of course Rex wanted a son 'to carry on the name,' as he sometimes explained it, but he never seemed to find anything but real pleasure in fathering girls, at the moment and forever. He and Mother finally produced David, but there was no change in the comfortable feeling Anne and Norah and I had about being there."

David, Norah, Anne, and MF,
ca. 1921.

MF, ca. 1923. "I am the first to
admit that one intoxicating angle
of my early eagerness to substitute
for the family cook on her day off
was the extra attention it brought
me. It made me feel creative and
powerful, and that is possibly the
truest reason for my continuing
preoccupation with the art of
eating."

MF and Norah, ca. 1925.

"When I was fifteen or sixteen I
was being deputized by my father
to substitute during vacations for
the Society Editor, the Gardens
and PTA man, and even the Sports
Editor. It's lucky for me that this
was in the summertime, when
almost nothing happened in
Whittier. I learned in my early
days, if I had not already known
it through my cells and bones as a
fifth-generation newswriter, that
there's never time to rewrite and
to consult the dictionary and to
brood or ponder.

"Father's paper went to press at
three in the afternoon, six days a
week, and my stuff had to be on
the copy-editor's spindle by one at
the latest. So all the time that I
was sharpening pencils for the
older reporters, and running
across the street to the dairy for a
pint of milk for my father, . . . my
mind was shaping sentences and
learning without even knowing it
to punctuate, and even to think, as
naturally as I breathed."

MF, ca. 1927, the year she traveled east to college by train, accompanied by her uncle Evans, Edith's brother.

"One time when he looked at me over his menu and asked me whether I would like something like a fresh mushroom omelet or one with wild asparagus, and I mumbled in my shy ignorance that I really did not care, he put down the big information sheet and for one of the few times in my life with him, he spoke a little sharply. He said, 'You should never say that again, dear girl. It is stupid, which you are not. It implies that the attentions of your host are basically wasted on you. So make up your mind, before you open your mouth. Let him believe, even if it is a lie, that you would infinitely prefer the exotic wild asparagus to the banal mushrooms, or vice versa. Let him feel that it matters to you...and even that he does!

"'All this,' my uncle added gently, 'may someday teach you about the art of seduction, as well as the more important art of knowing yourself.' Then he turned to the waiter and ordered two wild asparagus omelets. I wanted for a minute, I still remember, to leave the dining car and weep a little in the sooty ladies' room, but instead I stayed there and suddenly felt more secure and much wiser— always a heady experience but especially so at nineteen."

Sea Change

1929 — 1941

In 1929 the stock market crashed, and I got married for the first time and traveled into a foreign land across an ocean. All those things affected me, and the voyage perhaps most." So began M. F. K. Fisher's sensual and intellectual awakening. Under the tutelage of memorable landladies, waiters, and other French patriots, she was introduced to a European reverence for the table that would animate her "gastronomical me." While her husband, Al Fisher, pursued his doctorate in English literature at the university in Dijon, Mary Frances pursued life itself. "It was there, I now understand, that I started to grow up, to study, to make love, to eat and drink, to be me and not what I was expected to be."

Almost three years after arriving, the Fishers left France for home and a set of new and unwelcome constraints. California was in the full force of the Depression, and Al

and Mary Frances, like so many others, suffered a lack of work, a lack of money, a lack of privacy. (For two years, while Al looked for a job, they lived with the Kennedy family at the ranch and at the Laguna Beach cottage.) They had good friends, though, including Laguna neighbors Gigi and Dillwyn "Tim" Parrish who helped the couple fix up a much-needed place of their own near Occidental College, where Al took a position as an English instructor.

During the early days of Al's tenure at Occidental, Mary Frances spent time at the Los Angeles Public Library looking at old cookbooks and writing short, witty essays about her findings to show to Dillwyn Parrish, "a man destined to draw out anything creative in other people." (Fisher gave two accounts regarding whom she had in mind while writing the early gastronomical essays: in one she says they were written for Al, who to her annoyance showed the pieces to Dillwyn; the other cites Dillwyn as the original dedicatee. The distinction is without difference: Mary Frances had discovered, perhaps unconsciously as yet, her need to write *for* someone she loved.)

At Dillwyn's urging, Mary Frances put together a series of the essays and sent them to his sister, the novelist Anne Parrish, who in turn sent them to her editor, Gene Saxton at Harper & Brothers; Saxton shared the manuscript with the English publisher Hamish Hamilton. At a meeting with Hamilton and Saxton in London some months later, Mary Frances laughingly recollected, both men were dismayed to discover that M. F. K. Fisher was not a man, "and by the end of the long teatime we were planning fairly intelligently how best to get around the cold fact that nobody would believe that *Serve It Forth* had been written by a woman."

Mary Frances was in London at the time, by invitation of Dillwyn Parrish. Dillwyn had separated from his wife in 1935 and withdrawn to his family home in Delaware. He had maintained an involved correspondence with Mary Frances, however, and early in 1936 invited her to join him and his mother for two months in Europe. She went with Al's encouragement, surprised, not for the first time, by Al's willingness to be apart.

Al was uncertain and unhappy in his position at Occidental, and when Dillwyn suggested that both Fishers join him in Switzerland in the fall, they agreed. The three lived together in Vevey on the slopes above Lac Léman, and with the help of a local architect devised plans for the extensive renovation of an old house on the grounds called Le Pâquis. But the Fisher's marriage, already weakened by increasing estrangement between them, could not withstand the

attraction that drew Mary Frances and Dillwyn ever closer together. In 1937, Al and Mary Frances decided to separate, though they would not legally divorce until 1939.

Amidst the upheaval of Fisher's private life, *Serve It Forth* was published in England and America. "I was so involved emotionally that I paid no attention to it," she wrote, "and indeed I have never felt anything but a kind of withdrawal and regret, at the publication of any book or story I have ever written since."

Blissfully isolated with Dillwyn at Le Pâquis, Mary Frances passed a brief but intensely happy period in her life. Together they entertained friends, gardened, took walks, and co-wrote a novel, *Touch and Go*, that Harper's would publish under the pseudonym Victoria Berne. But the equanimity of those days would be short-lived. Late in the summer of 1938, Dillwyn was struck with an embolism that traveled up his left leg, requiring amputation. He spent months in Swiss hospitals, with more operations and much painful testing, and still his condition was unimproved. Nearly two years would pass before Dillwyn was diagnosed with Buerger's disease, a fatal circulatory illness. In the meantime he endured a grueling regimen of treatments that failed to relieve his pain more than briefly. "I was a woman condemned," Mary Frances wrote, "plucked at by demons, watching her true love die too slowly."

In 1940, with war threatening and Dillwyn worsening, the two left Switzerland and returned to California, where they married and bought the harsh, lovely southern California property they named Bareacres. There they would live until August of 1941 when Dillwyn, worn out by pain and the hopelessness of his condition, committed suicide.

MF and Al Fisher at the ranch, 1929.

MF on her wedding day, September 5, 1929. She and Al set sail for France soon after.

Alfred Young Fisher was conservative by nature if not by intention. The son of a Presbyterian minister, he was "consumed by a desire to be A WRITER." Though Al never achieved the renown he craved, he had a long and respected career as a teacher of English literature.

Before boarding the ship for France, 1929. MF found herself mysteriously, beneficently affected by sea travel, and would write eloquently of the "sea change" phenomenon in The Gastronomical Me.

Dijon, 1929. "There I was, standing in the center of the place d'Armes, which was in the center of Dijon, and therefore in the center of France itself. In other words, the whole world was mine."

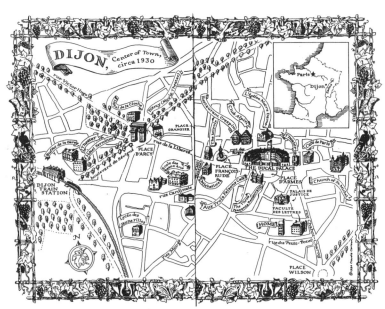

A personalized map of Dijon as it appeared in Long Ago in France *(1991).*

The rooftops of Dijon, 1938.

AUX TROIS FAISANS

The rue Chabot-Charny in Dijon housed the Faculté des Lettres and bordered the rue du Petit Potet, where Al and MF lived in a boardinghouse run, in succession, by the landladies Ollagnier and Rigoulot, both of whose habits, temperaments, and quirks provided MF a lasting source of amusement and fascination.

A sketch of Chef Racouchot at MF's beloved Trois Faisans, where she and Al, under the gentle instruction of the waiter Charles, ate "the biggest, as well as the most exciting, meal that either of us had ever had. . . . Even if we had never gone back and never learned gradually how to order food and wine, it would still be among the important [meals] of my life."

Dijon's church of Notre Dame as seen from the rue Musette in about 1930. "Dijon was really not a flowery city. It was ugly, as a matter of fact. The walls were always damp, and it was a gray, dim, dark town, very provincial. Of course, I loved it. I took it for granted, in a strange way."

MF and Lawrence Clark Powell in Dijon, ca. 1930. MF had been acquainted with Powell at Occidental, but in Dijon, where he and Al Fisher were working toward their doctorates in literature, "we started a fine relationship, which is still one of the best of my life. . . .

"As I remember, we used to buy a bottle of wine now and then at the little Spanish wine shop nearby, and Larry and Al and I would go up to Larry's room or to our little purple-lavender-brown rooms. We had an old phonograph, and we'd play records and talk about affairs and drink a bottle of Moulin à Vent 1928, which cost something like a dollar then."

Al in Dijon, ca. 1930.

The Kennedy siblings (from left): David, Norah, Anne, and MF. Whittier, June 1931. At Edith's suggestion, MF returned alone to California to spend the summer with her family. The separation seemed too easy for Al, and was a source of hurt and confusion to her. She went back to France at the end of the summer accompanied by Norah, then fourteen.

Georges Connes, who supervised Al's doctorate, would remain a lifelong friend of MF's.

MF with Norah, en route to
Dijon, at the Colonial Exposition
in Paris, August 1931.

Al and Lawrence Powell. Dijon, November 1931. "One time Al read that Rimbaud and Baudelaire drank Pernod. So he wanted to try it. It cost a lot, we thought, but he ordered it anyway, at the Café de Paris, where they served it properly... with water and no ice. It was properly milky and probably very strong, although it was not the prewar kind made with wormwood that ate one's brain away.

"But Al was convinced that his brain was being eaten away. One day Larry and I were walking home with him, and Al stopped and said, 'I see tiny gnomes rising between the cobbles in the street.' And Larry and I knew it was so phony that we broke out laughing. We knew that Al wanted to see little gnomes, because he had been drinking Pernod for three days. Oh well, one Pernod, two Pernod, but never a rotted mind like those of some of the late nineteenth-century poets whom he hoped to resemble one day. So Al went back to Vin Blanc d'Alsace and his coffee."

César, the Provençal village butcher, pouring wine for two fishermen while Lawrence Powell looks on. "César was all that every man wants secretly to be: strong, brave; foul, cruel, reckless; desired by women and potent as a goat; tender and very sweet with children; feared by the priest, respected by the mayor; utterly selfish and generous as a prince; gay. César was man. Man noble and monstrous again after so many centuries."

Al and MF with Lawrence Powell at Le Cros de Cagnes in Provence, before returning to America. "The next time we put to sea, in 1932, was not so much later, about a year...but I was more than a year older. . . . It was hard to leave Europe. But I knew that even if we stayed, our young days there were gone. The first insouciant spell was broken, and not by the act of buying tickets, as Al seemed to believe."

Laguna Beach, ca. 1930.

MF, Al, and Anne.

MF, home in Whittier, 1932.
"I was already beginning to have theories about what and how I would serve in my home.

"I was beginning to believe, timidly I admit, that no matter how much I respected my friends' gastronomic prejudices, I had at least an equal right to indulge my own in my own kitchen. (I am no longer timid, but not always adamant, when it is a question of religion or old age or illness.)

"I was beginning to believe that it is foolish and perhaps pretentious and often boring, as well as damnably expensive, to make a meal of four or six or eight courses just because the guests who are to eat it have always been used to that many. Let them try eating two or three things, I said, so plentiful and so interesting and so well cooked that they will be satisfied. And if they aren't satisfied, let them stay away from our table, and our leisurely comfortable friendship at that table.

"I talked like that, and it worried Al a little, because he had been raised in a minister's family and taught that the most courteous way to treat guests was to make them feel as if they were in their own homes. I, to his well-controlled embarrassment, was beginning to feel quite sure that one of the best things I could do for nine tenths of the people I knew was to give them something that would make them forget Home and all it stood for, for a few blessed moments at least."

MF and Al in Laguna, ca. 1932.

DILLWYN · ·GIGI·

MF and Al on the steps of the house at Eagle Rock, near Occidental College, ca. 1934.

Dillwyn and Gigi Parrish, ca. 1930. Dillwyn, nicknamed Tim, came from a family of artists and writers that included his cousin, the illustrator Maxfield Parrish.

Dillwyn would draw and paint throughout his life, but with particular intensity in the years preceding his early death. Gigi Parrish was married to Dillwyn at

the time they met the Fishers in Laguna Beach. She was pursuing a career as a film actress when she left him to marry the actor and writer John Weld.

The town of Vevey above Lac Léman, where MF, Al, and Dillwyn lived during the renovation of Le Pâquis.

MF marketing in Vevey, 1936.

The house and fountain at Le Pâquis before the renovation began.

"Un pâquis, *the French dictionary says, is a grazing ground or pasture. But when we bought our home in Switzerland, and found that it had been called Le Pâquis for several centuries by all the country people near it, we knew that it meant much more than 'pasture' to them. The word had a tenderness to it, like the diminutive given to a child or a pretty girl, like the difference between* lambkin *and* lamb. . . .

"*It was a sloping green meadow, held high in the air above the Lac Léman by stone walls. A brook ran through it under pollarded willows, and old trees of pears and plums and apples bent away from the pushings of the lake winds. The ancient soil was covered with a dazzling coat always, low and filled with violets and primulas and crocuses in the spring, waist-high with such flowers in summer as I have only seen like shadows in real gardens. . . .*

"*There was a fountain, too, near the road by the stone house.*

It had been there for longer than even the Federal maps showed, and people walking up the long pull from lake level knew it as well as they knew their mothers, and stopped always to drink and rest their backs from the pointed woven baskets they wore. Even after we came, and planted more trees and added rooms to the house, they continued to stop at the fountain, and that made us feel better than almost anything else."

"A worker digging up an old tree. This picture is good, because it is taken from the south-west end of the terrace and shows quite clearly the coast-line with the road below, and where our garden will be, along the wall."

MF and Dillwyn Parrish at Le Pâquis, ca. 1936.

"The walls are going up. Unlike Al, who seems capable of standing for hours watching the snail-pace of the work, I cannot enjoy it. It is ugly. I know it will be thoroughly done, since it is Swiss. There is no aid I can lend. So I prefer not to see it in its present cluttered hideous form. I think I seem unsympathetic to Al. I am sorry."

Vevey, 1937. Left to right: Dillwyn, Edith, MF, and Al.

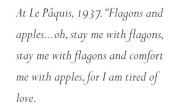

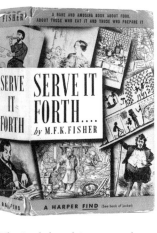

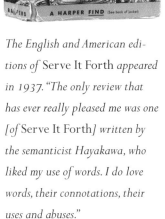

The English and American editions of Serve It Forth *appeared in 1937. "The only review that has ever really pleased me was one [of* Serve It Forth*] written by the semanticist Hayakawa, who liked my use of words. I do love words, their connotations, their uses and abuses."*

At Le Pâquis, 1937. "Flagons and apples... oh, stay me with flagons, stay me with flagons and comfort me with apples, for I am tired of love.

"Was that it? It was in the Bible. Did it say tired or sick?

I was tired. I wanted love, but I was tired of it, wearied by its involutions, convolutions, its complex intraplexities. I had fled from it, . . . the husk and the bud, the empty and the refilled, renewed, revived, recrucified...

" . . . Running away had not helped us at all. I loved [my husband] too much to lie, although not enough to live with him... and it was the same thing again: Stay me with flagons, for I am tired, sick, tired, tired of love."

The finished house, inside and outside, at Le Pâquis. "The part of the house we added to the little stone building was, I suppose, quite impractical for anyone but us. It disturbed and shocked the architect and all the contractors for floor and plumbing and such, because it was designed so that we, the owners of the place, could be its cooks and servants. That was not becoming to our station. We got what we wanted, though, and the kitchen and pantry were part of the living room... up and down a few steps, around a corner or two... so that music and talk and fine smells moved at liberty from one part to another."

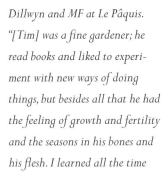

Dillwyn and MF at Le Pâquis. "[Tim] was a fine gardener; he read books and liked to experiment with new ways of doing things, but besides all that he had the feeling of growth and fertility and the seasons in his bones and his flesh. I learned all the time from him, and we worked together two summers in Le Pâquis. . . .

"Whenever we could stop gardening long enough to go down [to Vevey], things grew too fast for us. It was the oldest soil either of us had ever touched, and it seemed almost bursting with life, just as it was alive with insects and little creatures and a hundred kinds of worms waiting to eat what grew in it. We ran a kind of race with it, exciting and exhausting."

*Whittier, 1937. Left to right: Rex,
MF, Norah, Edith, Anne, and
David.*

34

At Le Pâquis, ca. 1938.
"My whole existence has become
more completely physical than
ever before in my life: I eat, sleep,
listen, even cook and read with
an intensity and a fullness that
I have never felt until now. I am
completely absorbed in myself—
but myself as seen through
Timmy."

Last idyllic days, in the summer
of 1938: a picnic in the meadow
at Le Pâquis, with Norah (left),
Dillwyn, and Anne Parrish. At
the end of that summer, Dillwyn
would be struck with the embolism
that caused him to lose his leg,
marking the first stage in his
fatal illness.

MF and Dillwyn in the dining
room at the Ritz in Paris, with
Anne Parrish to MF's right, and
a friend.

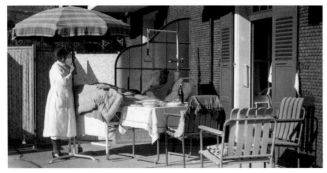

On the terrace of the Hotel Bärem in Adelboden after Dillwyn's first surgery, November 1938.

"I notice two things about this life, since the first night at the Bärem: my increased fastidiousness and my equally increased gour- mandise. *Since I can remember, I've been very clean, but now I spend long serious minutes, after my bath, drying each toenail; I wash my navel or my ears as if they were Belleek china teacups; a tiny hangnail sends me hurrying*

for scissors, oil, all the minutiae of a complete manicure. . . .

"I eat a lot of salad, on which I put a spoonful of meat juice with a strange voluptuous solemnity. I am interested in this slowness and this solemnity. I suppose it is a desire to escape, to forget time and the demands of suffering. . . .

"After a day part cloudy and part sunlit, light from behind the western mountains beams suddenly across the valley and brings my mountains close enough to lean against. The snow of seven nights ago melts fast, and cliffs I never dreamed of stand out with abrupt starkness from the white slopes, their rock sides cozy in the unexpected light. Lower down, the pine trees are oily green-black, clustered like plant lice in diminishing dots up the mountain. At the bottom, the foamy, dirt-white ice water rushes, with a steady hissing, to the warm valleys."

MF and Dillwyn on their ninety acres near the town of Hemet, in southern California. They named their place Bareacres after a penniless but contented landowner in **Vanity Fair,** and it was indeed bare, untillable, and hauntingly beautiful. In the years before he died there, Dillwyn "painted like a possessed devil, which he was, and he left many fine canvasses." Bareacres remained a source of inspiration and comfort for MF even after she sold it more than a decade later.

MF, Dillwyn, and Anne. Bareacres,
ca. 1940.

One of the paintings Dillwyn
made of MF.

Dillwyn on the porch at Bare-
acres. The porch wrapped around
the north and east sides of the
house. He and MF slept on the
porch facing east.

"Our land was bare! It rose in rough steep hills, with one deep canyon that split it down from the Rim of the World, its horizon, to the wide dead riverbed that was its northern boundary. . . . The place was covered with great harsh boulders, some of them bigger than a house. . . .

"In front of the house, which stood about a thousand feet up off the wide dry riverbed that separated us from Hemet Valley, the land was steep but with fewer big rocks, almost like a meadow, covered with sage and mesquite and low cactus. Across the river-bed, northward, between us and Mount San Jacinto, lay the flat valley land, rich with apricot orchards. It was neatly laid out with roads and little houses here and there, but we could see only a general kind of lush carpet, flow-ery in spring, then green, and then winter-silver. Hemet was west-ward, invisible."

Arnold Elliot, ca. 1941. "We stayed aloof from active life in Hemet while Tim was there, because we knew his time was short and he had a lot of painting to do. We made fine firm friends, though."

One of these friends was Arnold Elliot, of whom MF wrote: "He had been a desert rat for many years, the kind of shadowy drifting loner who becomes almost dust colored—protective coloration, it is called in toads and mice and serpents, and the few real desert rats I have met were the same.... His eyes were as hard and colorless as stone, except when they smiled at Tim and now and then toward me."

Dillwyn and Arnold, ca. 1941.

Bareacres, 1941.

"After Tim died, Arnold buried the little tin box of clinkers [Tim's ashes] under an enormous hanging rock. I said, 'Let's go up to the Rim of the World and let the winds catch them,' but he said, 'Nope,' and simply walked off. I knew it was all right, and went back to Bareacres and waited, and when he came back, we had a good nip of whiskey.

"[After Arnold left Hemet,] I never heard from him again, except that he is still clear and strong in my heart.

"That is the way Bareacres is, of course. I am told that the fine pure air that first drew us there, half mountain and half desert, is now foul with smog and that the rich carpet of fruit trees we looked down on is solid with RVs and trailer parks. . . . Crest Drive is lined with million-dollar villas, with the subdivision where Bareacres was . . . the most snobbish and stylish area between Palm Springs and Los Angeles.

"That is the way it is, I say, and I do not grieve or even care. . . . I have taken and been given more than can ever be known that is heartwarming and fulfilling forever from that piece of wild haunted untillable land we named Bareacres for a time."

Dillwyn, Bareacres, 1941.

As Far As the Flesh Allows

1942 — 1950

Dillwyn Parrish would remain the irreplaceable love of Fisher's life. As rending as his suffering had been, his death, when it came, hollowed her out. To survive him seemed impossible, and for a time she could do no more than shut out "the howling, hideous, frightful grief." But she resisted the undertow of her loss with a resoluteness that was astonishing for how quickly it took hold. Within a month after Dillwyn died, Mary Frances wrote in her journal, "I must stop this ghastly life of compromise and get to work. It is bad for me, this drifting about and postponing the truth: I must live alone. . . . I *am* alone, completely and unalterably. . . ."

Consider the Oyster, begun during Dillwyn's illness, was published just weeks after he died. An amusing and eloquent paean to oysters and oyster-eaters, the book was written in an attempt to distract Dillwyn from his pain; it was a great disappointment to Mary Frances that he never saw it. Soon after *Oyster* appeared, she wrote *How to Cook a Wolf.* "I did it in a few days, it seems to me now, as I walked up and down in Timmy's studio and dictated it to my sister Norah, who took it onto the typewriter. She was astonished by the smooth way it came out. I was still in strong grief and was beyond any feeling of surprise."

News of the war in Europe and speculation on the fate of friends there had deeply distressed Mary Frances and Dillwyn; and *How to Cook a Wolf* was fueled by her identification with wartime as well as private loss, and by her conviction that the thoughtful preparation of food and mindful eating were true ways to ward off hunger, hurt, or any other wolf at the door. Both books were well if not widely reviewed, and M. F. K. Fisher began to draw notice as a writer of distinction in a genre whose boundaries she would largely redefine.

Friends and family had suggested that Mary Frances not stay on alone at Bareacres. Financial straits and the threat of isolation prompted her to go to Hollywood, where she got a job as a screenwriter at Paramount Pictures. She quickly came to dislike the work and resent the town's social impositions—"the sterile creative life, living rather like a literary starlet, going to the right parties and so on." In spite of her ambivalence toward Hollywood, Mary Frances was rebuilding a life there when tragedy unseated her again. Just one year after Dillwyn's death, her brother David killed himself on the night before he was to enter the army. Rex and Edith seemed to draw apart in the wake of David's death, and the family pattern was irrevocably changed.

Not long after David's suicide, Mary Frances broke her contract with Paramount, and in the spring of 1943 she withdrew to Bareacres, pregnant with her first child. She had managed to keep her pregnancy a secret from even Rex and Edith, and when her daughter was born on August 15, 1943, all but her closest friends were told that Anne Kennedy Parrish was adopted. Mary Frances never revealed the father's identity. (Anne later changed her name to Anna, as it appears in the remainder of this book.)

At Bareacres, Mary Frances continued work she had begun in Hollywood on *The Gastronomical Me*. In a letter to a friend, she refers to her fear of writing, for the first time, "without Tim's cold judicial ear to listen." (She discounted *How to Cook a Wolf* as being mostly recipes.) Published in 1943, *The Gastronomical Me* is a memoir, arguably the finest of all her books, which she later described as "a very personal book, and since my first attempt to read it for the psychiatrist I've never even looked in it."

A precarious emotional state, the legacy of recent trauma, prompted Mary Frances to leave Bareacres again. In the spring of 1945 she traveled to New York for an indefinite stay, accompanied by Anna—then almost two—and longtime helper and Hemet neighbor Elsa Purdy. The first week there she met Donald Friede of the highly respected but short-lived publishing team Covici-Friede, "a dynamic and restless person who knew almost as much about publishing as he did about modern art and other forms of seduction." They were married two weeks later. Taking charge of her career, Donald broke all of Fisher's existing contracts and signed her with Viking, where his former partner Pascal Covici was now an editor, and with the man who would be her agent for nearly four decades, Henry Volkening. That summer in New York, energized by her sophisticated literary environs, Mary Frances began work on a collection of banquet lore, *Here Let Us Feast*. "The whole long summer was a dream of hard work and hard play. . . ."

Despite her misgivings about how Donald would occupy himself in the relative isolation of Bareacres, the Friedes moved back there in the fall of 1945. Mary Frances was pregnant with her second daughter, Kennedy, who arrived in March, some seven weeks premature. A difficult pregnancy had been further burdened by the pressures of her professional commitments and Donald's as yet unsuccessful relocation. Still, Mary Frances would complete four books in the next three years: the novel *Not Now but* Now, the translation of Brillat-Savarin's *Physiology of Taste,* and the work that would cap the eventual *Art of Eating* series, *An Alphabet for Gourmets.*

True to her fears, Donald did not thrive at Bareacres, and in the spring of 1948 he got an ill-fated job in Hollywood that forced their relocation to Los Angeles. Donald's job, developing literary projects for a film agency, would last a brief six weeks; the experience was altogether disastrous and Donald emerged from the failed enterprise in a state of near collapse. Reassembling her family and professional life at Bareacres, Mary Frances found herself unable to cope with Donald's debilitation. They decided to separate while he sought psychiatric help and then tried to reestablish himself as a literary agent; their separation ended in divorce in 1951.

Returning to Hollywood had taken an immeasurable toll on Mary Frances. In a journal entry dated July 27, 1947, she wrote of burning some twenty-five years' worth of notes and journals in the preceding weeks, sparing only a few entries, including those that held value as future story ideas and notes on Dillwyn's illness. For years she would revisit and question this act, reflecting on it in her journals as a kind of subconscious purgation—she would beat Hollywood to the task of reinventing herself by destroying a good part of her private history. She later regretted it enormously.

On May 9, 1949, Edith Kennedy died of illness related to heart disease. Mary Frances moved back to the Whittier ranch that fall to help Rex with the running of the household; she and the girls remained there with him until his death in June of 1953.

In the month after Dillwyn's death, MF wrote in her journal, "I try to live (even asleep?) with what dignity I can muster, but I wonder if there is much in this abject procedure. I write it down here partly because this is the first night I am really alone and partly to shame myself, like a whiplash. I can hear a night dove in the arroyo, and Freda van Benschoten's spaniel, whose voice has just changed, barks heavily across the flats. I shall live, I know in spite of myself, and where and how?"

With Norah, David, and his wife Sarah. Mexico, 1941.

"One morning we were sitting after breakfast around the big cluttered table, when there was a strange dreadful sound outside on the street, and a wailing cry.... A woman from the hills with a big pot of boiled beans on her head had stumbled, there in front of our house on her way to sell them in the market. She had probably walked most of the night. And they were probably her whole crop, David said.

"The beans, pale and nasty, were spread on the stones, all mixed with broken pottery and already half-eaten by the starved dogs of the village and a few beggar-children. People walking to market made a wide silent circle, or hurried past sadly, impotently. And the hill-woman sat folded into her shawl, with her face on her knees, never making any sound after her first wail.

"She sat there all day, not moving even her shoulders, with one closed hand beside her on the cobbles.

"The beans were soon gone, and someone picked up the broken clay into a little pile, so that the street looked cleaner than before, where the dogs had licked around her.

"At lunch we could not eat or sing or talk. We did not speak of the woman sitting there, but each of us would go secretly from the others to the upper windows, on tiptoe, and peek to see her. None of us knew what to do, in the face of such absolute stillness....

Bareacres, ca. 1942.

"And at sundown she was gone. None of us saw her go. She took all the pieces of clay with her, back to the hills. We could go out past the place where she had been, then, to eat some supper. We went to the Nido, and spent a lot of money, and drank cocktails first by the lake, still feeling shocked by the sound of the pot falling on the stones, and her long silence. It was her own kind of flight, as good perhaps as mine..."

First editions of Consider the Oyster *and* How to Cook a Wolf. *"I remember that I wrote a sad little criticism to my new editor, Sam Sloan . . . about how I wished that I'd been notified earlier that [Consider the Oyster] would be published, because neither Timmy nor I knew about it and I very mistakenly felt, for a few minutes anyway, that he might have put off dying, if he'd known the publication date. . . . I dedicated the book to him, and I began to realize then that I must always write toward somebody I love, to make it seem real."*

About How to Cook a Wolf, *MF wrote, "it seemed quite natural to do a good book exactly as I would do a good report for Father's paper, to earn my living in the only way I could. This was probably the first time I was aware of writing to pay my way, and it may have helped keep everything so clear and fast."*

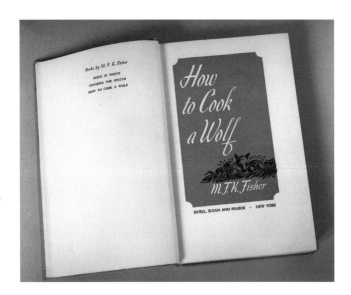

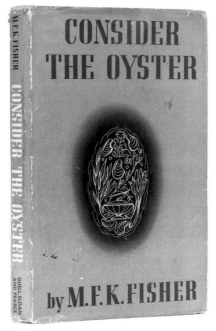

Publicity photos, 1942. After seeing her picture alongside a review of How to Cook a Wolf, *Paramount executives attempted to "discover" MF for the screen instead of the page, but she declined.*

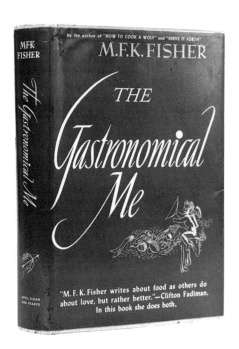

A first edition of The Gastronomical Me. *MF dedicated the book "to my sister Anne Kennedy Kelly, who was two years younger than I and always a complex and fascinating person."*

Anne and MF, ca. 1942.

"The prettifiers of human passion choose to think that a man who has just watched his true love die is lifted above such ugly things as food, that he is exalted by his grief, that his mind dwells exclusively on thoughts of eternity and the hereafter. . . .

"The truth is that most bereaved souls crave nourishment more tangible than prayers: they want a steak. What is more, they need a steak. Preferably they need it rare, grilled, heavily salted, for that way it is most easily digested, and most quickly turned into the glandular whip their tired adrenals cry for. . . .

"Underneath the anguish of death and pain and ugliness are the facts of hunger and unquenchable life, shining, peaceful. It is as if our bodies, wiser than we who wear them, call out for encouragement and strength and, in spite of us and of the patterns of proper behavior we have learned, compel us to answer, and to eat."

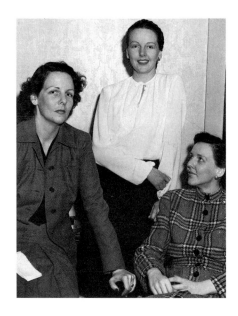

After Anna's birth, Bareacres, September 1943. "Anne is right in every way. She is a healthy, impish little being with merry dark eyes. And now my life seems full and warm and rich again. I was out in the cold for a long time."

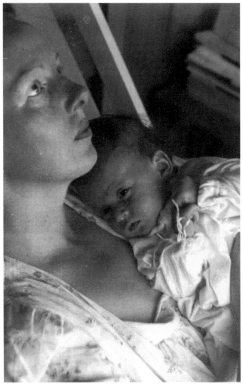

At the ranch, December 26, 1943, the day of Anna's christening. MF with her sisters Anne (left) and Norah; MF and Anna with Rex and Edith.

Bareacres, December 1944. MF
with Anna.

The actress Gloria Stuart, a good
friend from Laguna days.

A globe decoupaged with images
of MF's "world" made for her by
Gloria Stuart. The globe was
among her treasured belongings.

MF and Donald Friede on the day they were married, Atlantic City, May 1945. "As for dining-in-love, I think of a lunch at the Lafayette in New York, in the front café with the glass pushed back and the May air flowing almost invisibly over the marble tabletops, and a waiter named Pons, and a bottle of Louis Martini's Folle Blanche and moules more-or-less-marinières but delicious, and then a walk in new black-heeled shoes with white stitching on them beside a man I had just met and a week later was to marry, in spite of my obdurate resolve never to marry again and my cynical recognition of his super-salesmanship."

Donald Friede, 1946.

Donald, Anna, Elsa Purdy, and ME. New York City, July 1945. "We had a summer lease on a duplex down on Bank Street in the Village. Every morning I walked in the cool bright air to Fifth Avenue, where I either went on walking, or rode on top of one of the grand old buses, to the Public Library. I would work [on Here Let Us Feast*] all day in the big reading room, with lunch often at exciting places, and then a late afternoon glass of white wine in the gardens of the Museum of Modern Art while I waited for Donald. We would walk or ride in the breathless summer twilight, to dine with people in their high apartments or down in the Village in the sidewalk restaurants. The whole long summer was a dream of hard work and hard play. . . ."*

MF's agent, Henry Volkening (right), with his friend and business partner Diarmuid Russell in the early forties. "For some thirty-eight years Henry Volkening was what is too casually called my literary agent. . . . Henry was a small man, I remember, and a real gent, . . . determined that I would never write a best-seller in my life. . . . He hated my working for 'women's magazines,' especially doing easy monthly essays about potato salad and somesuch. . . . and I know that he was very happy indeed when I stopped supporting myself and the children by their monthly demands. . . .

"Henry was cool about my earning anything at all, really. One year, I made $37.50. This pleased him enormously, and as he meticulously took out his own 10 percent and pocketed it before sending the rest on to me, he announced that we had finally got down to real business with the Martini Fund. . . . We kept up its somewhat flexible level even when we both knew that we'd long since exhausted it on my annual trips to New York."

MF's editor at Viking, Pascal Covici, in 1953. "Pascal Covici, who ended his long life as one of the last of the 'true breed' of editors, started it in Chicago as part-owner of one of those mysteriously potent bookstores that happen in places like Paris and Budapest, and even in Los Angeles when someone like Jake Zeitlin is there... or in any smaller town where eager impatient minds must seek out good talk. In Covici's correctly shabby, dusty rendezvous, stripling giants like Theodore Dreiser and Ben Hecht decided the future of the world. Then Pat moved on to New York, to be half of what soon became a prestigious publishing firm, Covici-Friede."

With Donald and Edith in Whittier, 1945. MF was pregnant with her daughter Kennedy at the time.

Kennedy's birth announcement in the Hemet News, *and the medical bill for her delivery.*

STATEMENT
Pasadena Lutheran Hospital
1845 N. Fair Oaks Ave.
Phone SYcamore 7-113

Pasadena, Calif., Apr 24, 46

In account with Baby Friede

For Services Rendered

Hospital Service from 3-17 to 3-25		Paid
March 25 to Apr 24	30 days @ 4.00	120 00
Operating Room Fee		
Anesthetic Drugs		
Oxygen		
Laboratory Fee		
Pathological Fee		
X-Ray		
Physio-therapy		
Pharmacy Supplies	Paid in full	
Medical Supplies	Thank you	
Surgical Supplies	F. Lowert	
Cast		
Baby Friede Formula		
3 oz milk		
2 oz water		
1 rounded teaspoon		120 00
raw sugar		

Donald with Kennedy Friede at seven weeks. Bareacres, May 1946.

MF and Donald on her thirty-eighth birthday, July 3, 1946. With the complications of her pregnancy behind her, MF seemed to revel in her children. "We are in debt, which I hate as much as I always have. I refuse to feel grim about it, because I know that we can and will get out of it and meanwhile we are happy and healthy. What fine children we have! I know I'd seem dull and smug if anyone got me to talk about them, but that is how I feel...that they are completely delightful and satisfying crea-tures, pleasant to look at, smell, touch, listen to, watch, kiss, feed, clean." She found less to be enthu-siastic about in her work, however. Here Let Us Feast *was lan-guishing in the marketplace; she was ambivalent about the novel nearly finished,* Not Now but Now*; and she suffered feelings of inadequacy about the Brillat-Savarin translation she had begun: "The problem of the waver-ing values of words frightens me." (The translation of* The Physiol-ogy of Taste, *when it was com-pleted, pleased MF enormously.)*

Kennedy was christened at the ranch on September 15, 1946, the same day as her cousin, John Barr Jr., born to John and Norah Kennedy Barr. From left: Anne Kennedy Kelly holding Kennedy, Norah and John Barr, Anna, Sean Kelly holding John Jr., Edith, MF, and Rex.

With Kennedy.

MF and Rex, October 1945. Some months after the publication of Here Let Us Feast *(1946, a year and a half after these pictures were taken), MF wrote a letter to Rex calling his attention to the fact that he had never said anything to her about the book. She had struggled against health, family, and professional difficulties to finish the job, and it hurt her deeply that Rex acknowledged neither her perseverance nor its product. "I have always felt that you considered me a little lazy or careless," she wrote, "and all the time I was slugging away to finish this last book I kept thinking how much it would please you to know that I could do what I set out to. What you think of me is one of the most important parts of my existence... as you can see by this note which after much thought I feel I must write to you!" The letter was not sent, and in a postscript to herself MF continued: "Father because of David's death has withdrawn from his other three children. . . . It is a sad thing. . . . Our love and respect . . . could so well solace him, in part at least, for the abrupt break in a glass that might otherwise have stayed flawed and fearful for a long time...."*

MF and Kennedy on the patio at
Bareacres, October 1946.

Man Ray cutting Anna's hair.
Bareacres, October 1946. Man
Ray had a complex and somewhat
strained friendship with Donald,
but of her own relationship with
the artist MF said, "we understood
each other completely, but never
much with words."

Pictures from the summer and fall of 1947. "I am keeping a Line-a-Day book! . . . because we started having so many kittens, puppies, fish, and so on, and I'd forget important dates about them. And then I remembered how Mother used to keep that kind of book, that has space for five years, and how on looking through one a few years ago I had a strange good feeling of solidity and strength, from seeing that filled page without pain and for the most part without passion, marking the weather and the number of new-laid eggs."

MF and the girls in front of their Los Angeles home, spring 1948. In letters to friends and in her journal, MF had written about the approaching relocation with guarded optimism, "a kind of horrified excitement." She would later retract her optimism, but not her sense of horror at the anticipated move.

An Alphabet for Gourmets *was published in 1949. "I've always been pleased by the strange little drawings Marvin Bileck did for it. I dedicated the Alphabet to Hal Beiler, who had been my doctor for a long time, and who kept a kind and loving eye on me for another twenty-five or thirty years."*

(At left and above) The Friedes after their return to Bareacres midyear in 1948.

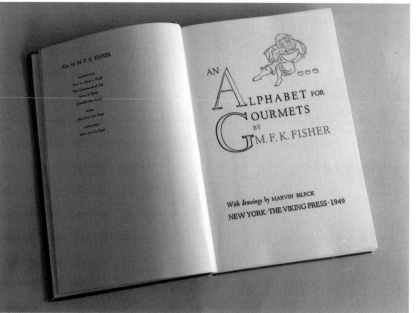

MF at Bareacres, ca. 1948. "It is two years ago now, not one, that I carried some twenty-five years of notes and such-like to the incinerator. . . . I am not quite sure why. I had no fear of harmful indiscretions in what I had written...such revelations were more of the mind than of the heart, with me, and so could harm nobody but myself. But I was in an almost death-like state: we were about to go to live in Hollywood and Donald was to work for Ralph Blum. . . . I felt that my life as I had tried to live it up to that time was over... everything I had learned from Dillwyn and other good people must be put aside... I must readjust my ways of eating and drinking and feeling and behaving and thinking and judging... It is a wonder I did not sell Bareacres and have my hair dyed and give up MFK Fisher and so on and so on, to make a completer change. Burning the journals was, I suppose, a kind of symbolic sacrifice. And then it was to no good! In six months we were back here, broke and broken. I think now I should have kept what I had written. It was of my essence, no matter how dull, and I poured it upon the ground. When most people die, they are ash and dust but still exist in the hearts and minds of those who knew them, the way Mother does in mine, and how many others! But when I died, there in the incinerator, nobody knew but me, and it is very lonely to mourn what no other person ever knew." (1949)

With Anna, Kennedy, and Elsa Purdy. Bareacres, ca. 1949. "I see the children curving up into the spiritual air like fern-fronds, shaped by their own mysterious natures and the winds and the worms, and I wonder that I dare peck at them, to turn them this way or that in their inevitable growth. But I must."

At the ranch, ca. 1950. "Well, I see now what people have long told me, that I am intrinsicately [sic] strong. . . . What does excite me is that finally I begin to feel shadows or premonitions or hints of my potential strengths. My god...what shall I do with myself, if I should live so long? Not politics. I'd like to remake the world's thinking there, but I am not that ageless. I want very much to draw, sculpt, fashion with my hands. But the only thing I know about is writing, and given my passion for the clear right meaning of words I should perhaps learn more of them...semantics...the ability to make simple people care about what they say...I am clearly a teacher, a preacher. To many good people including myself I am objectionable, being thus the mentor. Hell and its angels, I can not do otherwise than instruct, guide, lead, boss. Once I get over this period of uncertainty in my soul, I'll be invincible, as far as the flesh allows."

"Insolite"

1951 — 1970

The situation in which Mary Frances now found herself—back in Whittier after so many years, running Rex's household and single-parenting two young girls—was not one she had envisioned. In addition to her responsibilities at home, she was propelled by Rex's failing health into a part-time position at the newspaper, a job complicated by the difficulties of being both M. F. K. Fisher and the boss's daughter. In what little time remained, she struggled to meet deadlines for the various magazines that provided her chief source of income. With Donald Friede's shepherding—he continued to take an interest in Mary Frances as a writer of great talent—*The Art of Eating* collection was published in 1954 by World Book, where he was then an editor. Fisher would not publish another book until *A Cordiall Water* in 1961.

Emotionally drained by the failure of her marriage, troubled by Rex's increasing withdrawal as well as her own acute sense of aloneness, Mary Frances fell into depression. She began seeing a psychiatrist to cope with what she called "the black chill of exhaustion and emotional hysteria." And though she would never again be entirely free from bouts of depression, she would learn much about weathering their recurrence.

With Rex's blessing, Mary Frances had made the decision not to stay on in Whittier after his death but to sell the paper and the ranch and begin a new life elsewhere. When Rex died in June of 1953, she and the girls moved to St. Helena in northern California's Napa Valley, a town that would be her home base for almost twenty years. "I seem to go instinctively toward the vineyards!" she wrote. St. Helena "has unusually interesting people in it, either fourth and fifth generation French and Italian wine growers or people like me who have chosen this life rather than a more hectic and perhaps 'successful' one in big cities." She had also determined how she wanted to raise Anna and Kennedy: "By letting my girls see-smell-touch-speak outside our own borders I am helping them be thinking and good and loyal Americans." So, for the girls' sake and for her own, she took them to Aix-en-Provence in the summer of 1954. She was unhanding herself from the depression still, but over time France seemed to restore Mary Frances to herself and she thrived watching the girls adopt the country in their own ways.

In Aix, Mary Frances installed Anna and Kennedy in the home of a French family for several months while they learned the language and went to school. She lived nearby in the boardinghouse of Madame Lanes, a dispassionate and dignified survivor (of war, of change, of life itself) about whom she would write, "This old lady had almost as much to do with my development as did [my mother]." In the spring, making "a brutal rude switch in all our orderly lives," Mary Frances and the girls moved to the château grounds of Le Tholonet outside Aix. The nonacademic education Anna and Kennedy were getting in the company of the local farm families convinced Mary Frances to keep the girls out of school. The vacation spirit must have taken hold of her as well; to her surprise she found herself working on a children's story about an Aixois dog, not the biography of Madame Récamier long promised to Viking. (The children's story would appear many years later as *Boss Dog*; the book on Récamier would never materialize.)

In spite of serious misgivings, Mary Frances and her girls left Provence for California in July 1955. The decision was clouded not only by the idea of leaving, but also by the uncertain prospects of homecoming. They moved to San Francisco first, but "it was not at all right: the children were at the wrong ages, and I spent my time cooking and working, with no fun at all for any of us... a dreadful thing to happen in that wonderful town!" Moving back to St. Helena, she bought the house on Oak Avenue where she would spend most of the next fifteen years. "Life was really fine, divided between the little California town that was immediately home to us, and the older places in a much older world." Mary Frances and the girls picked up where they had left off, resuming their lives in the closely knit school and town.

In 1959, the three set off again for Europe, this time to Lugano, Switzerland, a mostly Italian-speaking town in the Ticino, where the girls were enrolled in boarding school. Donald Friede and his wife of eight years, Eleanor Kask Friede, joined them for several weeks of travel during the Christmas holidays, and an already good relationship between Eleanor and Mary Frances was cemented. When it was time to leave Lugano some months later, Mary Frances and the girls, Francophiles all, made a spur-of-the-moment decision to go back to Aix where, Mary Frances wrote, "we seemed to have left large parts of our human significance." During their several-month residence in and around Aix, she wrote *A Cordiall Water*. Considering it her best writing, Mary Frances would maintain unequaled affection for the slim book of folk remedies.

Early in 1961, she brought the girls home so they could finish their schooling within the American system. "The second time we left Aix was at once easier and more prolonged: I knew what I was doing, at least somewhat more clearly, and I could salve myself with the knowledge that I had returned once, and therefore might again."

A sense of ease in her surroundings, so natural to Mary Frances in Europe, seemed to elude her during this next decade in America, bringing as it did a series of physical and emotional displacements. In the fall of 1961 Anna, by then eighteen years old, went to New York to study acting; the following year Kennedy went away to boarding school, a decision precipitated by her mother's poor health. For nearly six months in 1962, Mary Frances was plagued by respiratory problems, often bedridden with pain and fatigue; her doctors' diagnoses were troublingly inconclusive. Illness, together with the girls' absence and the death of a beloved cousin, undermined her sense of purpose — and her own work was insufficient to fill the void. The journals Mary Frances kept throughout the sixties attest to recurring spells of depression; the number of residences she exchanged likewise point to an overriding restlessness.

Still she managed to work. While commuting between Berkeley and St. Helena (she was undergoing medical treatments in both places), Mary Frances researched and wrote *The Story of Wine in California* (University of California Press, 1962). The house on Oak Avenue remained her home base, but she found it increasingly difficult to work there. Over the next several years she would remove herself to a number of retreats, ranging from a hotel room in St. Helena to a rented cottage near her sister Anne's house in Genoa, Nevada. The wild and unfamiliar landscape of Nevada provided needed refuge, and Mary Frances laid out much of her personal geography of Aix,

Map of Another Town, in the isolation of a Nevada winter. That book would be published by Little, Brown & Company in 1964.

In the summer of 1964, after Kennedy's graduation from high school, Mary Frances went to Mississippi to teach American literature and English composition to the all-black student body at The Piney Woods School. She seemed to be searching for direction and her decision was met with varying degrees of consternation and admiration from the people in her immediate circle. But Mary Frances genuinely abhorred the divisiveness that characterized race relations in America and, inspired by the efforts and aims of the civil rights movement, she committed her creative energies to the school. In a letter to an editor at *The Saturday Evening Post* proposing an article she hoped to write about the experience, she outlined her reasons for going there: "I am preoccupied, absorbed really, in the problem of communication between people. That is why I am here, primarily: to help people articulate clearly their thoughts, needs, hopes. The lack of communication between Negroes and whites is one of the most shocking and dangerous things in our present world, to my mind. Without command of a common language *all* of us may well be damned, or so I believe deeply and honestly. And now I am here at one of the main sources of our misunderstandings, seeing and hearing every minute the results of generations of enforced illiteracy and inarticulacy . . . with people who are trying the way these Piney Woods students and teachers are, to escape into the light."

Her teaching schedule was more demanding than Mary Frances had envisioned, but also more fully engaging. And though she found it hard to keep up with professional commitments, such as her new position reviewing cookbooks for *The New Yorker*, she showed no qualms about the shift in her priorities. Taking a temporary leave of absence midyear to attend to family matters, Mary Frances was dismayed to find herself not invited back—apparently because of political differences over how the school should be run. The rejection was a blow to her, and she never wrote about Piney Woods for *The Saturday Evening Post* or any other publication.

When plans to teach foundered, Mary Frances chose to return to Nevada, again renting a small house close to her sister Anne's. There she tried to reconcile herself to twin blows of rejection, the one from Piney Woods, the other from her daughter Anna. Personal problems had precipitated a series of crises in Anna's life, and her inability at the time, along with her mother's, to bridge emotional differences hurt and bewildered them both. In the remaining weeks of winter, Mary Frances veered toward despair; she pulled herself back, as before, by sheer force of will and was home in St. Helena when she received news of Donald Friede's death in May. Three months later she would lose her sister Anne to cancer.

As was her pattern after times of sadness and stress, Mary Frances entered a phase of considerable productivity. Toward the end of 1965 she accepted an offer from William Targ, then an editor at Putnam, to write what would eventually become the distinctly personal "recipe book" *With Bold Knife and Fork*. It would not be published until 1969, after most of the pieces had appeared in her *New Yorker* column, "Gastronomy Recalled." In the spring of 1966 she presented a series of lectures for the University of California, "a hurried but well-documented survey of the history of gastronomy, as a kind of mirror of civilization." Soon thereafter, she agreed to write the text for Time-Life's *The Cooking of Provincial France*. The book was to be the first in a Foods of the World series; Julia Child and the writer and food consultant Michael Field were to be its consulting editors. Fisher left for France in June, going first to Paris to work with a photographer on the book's picture sequence. There she stayed in a hotel on the Seine where, years before, she and Dillwyn Parrish had intended to rent connecting rooms, making "a kind of pied-à-terre, a place where we could leave books and be warmer than in Switzerland. This all turned impossible, and when I went back so much later I felt scared, so that I asked to take one of those familiar rooms. And in the other, to my astonishment, lived a person I admired deeply named Janet Flanner." In a short time the two became strong friends, and though their future meetings would be brief and infrequent, their mutual admiration remained intact for the rest of their lives.

Fisher left Paris for Provence to meet Michael Field, who with his wife Frances was gathering recipes in the area. The three made Plascassier the base for their culinary excursions, staying by invitation at the home of Julia and Paul Child. The Childs were not in France during Fisher's stay, but they established an instant rapport upon meeting some weeks later in Boston.

Publication of the Time-Life book in 1968 stands as a kind of benchmark for Fisher's entry into the food establishment that included Julia Child, Craig Claiborne, and

James Beard. It was Child who encouraged Fisher's meeting with Judith Jones at Knopf, a publishing house Mary Frances had long admired. With Judith Jones as her editor, Mary Frances would publish several books there, beginning in 1970 with the childhood memoir *Among Friends*.

The natural elegance of *Among Friends* belies the difficulty Mary Frances had writing the book. She spent the first three months of that year sequestered on Long Island, severe winter weather forcing isolation beyond the seclusion she had desired. "I sweated like a stevedore, literally, over the actual turmoil that I'd made for myself, because I was determined to prove that most of us do not remember the real facts of something from our childhood, but instead recall what we were told we remembered by our parents and teachers. It was hard as Hell itself to strip down all the wishful dreams of what had really happened."

Released from Long Island, having accomplished what she set out to do, Mary Frances returned to St. Helena "to go back to my own cave... lick my new wounds... clear my wits if any." She began to think about selling her Oak Avenue home. The large three-floor Victorian was difficult to maintain by herself, and she saw less and less reason for doing so. When a friend from neighboring Sonoma Valley, David Pleydell-Bouverie, invited her to build a house on his land, she accepted, "especially since he proposed designing it for me. And this *he* did, with all the bold skill of his earlier days as an English architect, and his knowledge of the winds and weather of this country as an American rancher. I said I wanted two rooms and a big bath, with an arch at each end to repeat the curved doors of his two big barns. I wanted tile floors. He did not blink... and I went back to Aix for several months to grow used to a new future."

Pictures taken at the ranch between 1951 and 1952 with Rex, his three daughters, Norah, Anne, and MF, and his granddaughters, Anna and Kennedy. "I had decided to move to the Ranch from Bareacres because I knew I could not raise the two girls alone," MF wrote many years later, "and Rex needed me, and I needed Rex, and the girls needed Rex."

At the typewriter with Kennedy.

Norah, Rex, MF, and friend
Harold Price in San Francisco,
January 1951. Rex preferred that
MF didn't invite her "gentlemen
friends" to the ranch. (She seemed
to agree, in theory, anyway, that
discretion surrounding her divorce
and her children was called for.)
Getting away was often hard to
manage, and the practical difficulties of maintaining a social
life from Whittier exacerbated her
sense of isolation.

A gathering of friends and family at the ranch in 1950: Anne,
Norah, Rex, and MF form the core
of the group. MF's good friend
June Eddy is seated to Rex's left.

In the back row, third from the
left, is Nancy Jane "Nan" Newton;
her husband Charles is on her
right. Nan was MF's cousin and
"by mere chance," she wrote, "one of
the dearest friends of my life." She
dedicated Map of Another Town
to Nan.

Ca. 1952. "I find myself going back with astonishing clarity . . . to my youngest years. Of course this is largely because I am once more living in Whittier. I am so surprised to find myself even writing *that fact that I must look at it on the paper and say it to myself again, for of all the unplanned unexpected turns in my life, this is the most so. (I came Nov. 11, 1949. This is May 16, 1952.) For a long time I did not realize that I was here, really. Then I began to protest, and gave myself a rough year or so, filled with black moments of panic and despair. . . . And by now . . . I am in spite of myself behaving in a way usually confined to the very old, and going back into my past in this little town, plainly in order to make the present more accept-able to myself. In the wheelchair of my enforced presence here I run like a colt down the unpaved streets; I skin my knees once more and with an even sharper pain, with even brighter blood, upon the few sidewalks we had to skate on, almost forty years ago. I skoot [sic] down the grassy hills in an orange crate for a sled, where prim villas crowd now, and I fight and sing and tumble with a gang of children who are gone or dead or bald long since. Now and then I see one of them hereabouts, and I feel a kind of mirth, to hold the mirror of them up to my own tired eyes and greying hair. It has happened, I say. It has actually happened to us."

Christmas 1952.

MF and her sisters with and without children in 1953, their last summer at the ranch. "After Rex died, we moved to Northern California, with his full blessing. At first he had been disappointed to learn of my decision to sell the paper after he died. It would have been a cinch, as he himself assured me, to stay on as editor in the town where he'd been a respected citizen for some forty-two years.

What he did not realize was that what had been a little town of less than five thousand people when he moved there in 1911 was now a sprawling suburb of Los Angeles with several hundred thousand people calling it their headquarters. I felt no real emotional ties to it, and I was determined not to let my children breathe any more polluted air than they'd already absorbed. So we had the ranch

house bulldozed to the ground; now a wading pool is there for other children, in a little park that Rex left in perpetuity so that the old men of the suburbs would have a place to meet and youngsters would have a place to play. And we pulled up stakes completely and settled in St. Helena, with never a moment's regret."

The Red Cottage in St. Helena,
where MF moved with the girls in
1953.

Kennedy, MF, and Anna, ca. 1954.
"I knew, the first time I ever
smelled the pure sweet air as I
drove from Napa to St. Helena,
that I would live there. That was
during the Second World War,
when I was given a 'tour of the
wine country' by some friends
in San Francisco. We stopped in
Napa at a dark old bar that out-
of-towners have always found
quaint, and then, warmed by
unaccustomed morning tipples,
headed due north, up a true valley
that gradually tapered to its end
at the base of the great topless
mountain, and I knew I would be
back. And several years and a
marriage and a divorce and two
little girls later, I was. We were."

Anna and Kennedy on the Dutch ship Diermerdyk, *en route to France. August 1954.* "A part of me would withdraw with respect before the knowledge that there on the little ship, as everywhere, I could not even guess at the lives my children led."

On the Cours Mirabeau, Aix, 1954.

"The main street, which is called the most beautiful one in the world, . . . is very wide, with two double lines of giant plantains (*Platanus gigantum????*) which have been pollarded, so that they form a long green tunnel, or cave, and then in the winter a kind of shadowy drifting light, so that you feel like a fish in a beautiful pond. Everybody meets there on the Cours Mirabeau for everything... old women knit and watch the babies, students stroll and flirt and argue, business is transacted. . . . I cross it at least four times a day, and walk up and down it, and so far I have never failed to experience a kind of spiritual shudder-quiver-thrill at its peculiar beauty."

With Anna in the window of the Café Madeleine in Aix-en-Provence. MF and the girls would go there every Thursday for couscous.

The Château de Tholonet, about four miles north of Aix toward Mont Sainte-Victoire. In the spring of 1955, MF rented an apartment above the stables on the château grounds. "We have three little bedrooms and an ancient beautiful kitchen where we'll eat...big cool stone stable below."

Anna and Kennedy at Le Tholonet, summer 1955. "I meant to put the children in the public school here (one room, 6 grades, 26 pupils, one eccentric aged schoolmistress...) but they are so happy and blooming that I've said the hell with it. They get up when they want to, and either go down to the brook and wash some clothes with the farmer's wife and the shepherd's wife, chatter chatter chatter, or they go out into the meadows, now blazing with scarlet poppies and a hundred other flowers, with the shepherd and his 200 sheep, his rams, his goats with bells on their necks, and his three remarkable dogs named Venise, Matelot, and Kikize. Now and then he gives them a swig of wine from his bottle, or a slice of his onion or sausage, and they come home reeking and fall into bed for another good twelve hours."

Anna and Kennedy, ca. 1955.
"Things being as they are, I want
the children to grow up with fixed
roots and loyalties and reasons,
and I honestly believe that they
stand the best chance of turning
into good people as Americans...
with *the widest view I can man-*
age to give them of other people
and other viewpoints and other
ways of being rooted and loyal
and reasoning."

Paul Cézanne, Mont Sainte-
Victoire, *1902–04.*

On the Route de Saint-Antonin
near Le Tholonet with Mont
Sainte-Victoire in the back-
ground."That was where Cézanne
had lived and worked, and [Anna
and Kennedy] were his intimates,
in a strange way I never ques-
tioned. The first day we walked
out from Aix along the Route du
Tholonet and sat under a big pine
to wait through a passing autumn
rain, and they pointed out seri-
ously to me that the cracks in the
bark of the old tree were packed
with pigments, where someone had
scraped a palette, and then told
me that HE had left them there. I
never argued their acceptance of
the painter's presence. (How could
anyone, living under the Mont
Ste.Victoire?)"

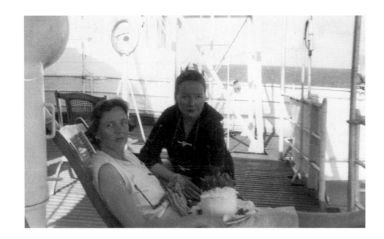

With Norah on board an Italian ship headed for America, 1955. (Norah and her children had spent the summer in Europe, and returned to America with MF and the girls.) "I was feeling disturbed and confused about ending, of my own volition, a period of great peace in our lives."

San Francisco, ca. 1957.

In the kitchen on Oak Avenue, ca. 1958.

The three-floor Victorian on Oak Avenue in St. Helena where MF would live on and off for almost fifteen years. "People grew used to the fact that the outside [of the] house would look shaggy and shabby while we lived there, and they came to feel easy within it. Outside, it was a soft faded mus-tard color, half-hidden by care-fully controlled masses of Peking bamboo. Inside, it was a charmed mixture of light and color, where the air was always sweet and the leaves made fine delicate curtains against the wavery old glass in the tall windows."

In the basement, ca. 1959.
"Part of the space turned into a
kind of wine-cellar pub, and there
were beds for four people, like
couches, in other stony places. . . .
There were books everywhere on
the wonderful wide ledges. . . .
Much of our time . . . was spent
down there. It was fine for good
bashes and dinner parties and
meetings. It was easy to bring edi-
bles down from the kitchen, and
the wine was already there! . . .
I found myself working more and
more in the basement, so that fi-
nally everything I was pondering
on was down there, close beside the
bed I grew to prefer to all others
in the lighter rooms upstairs."

Norah and MF, St. Helena, ca.
1959. The two sisters' lives were
closely entwined throughout their
adult years. They would weather
much together and remain friends
and frequent companions.

The town of Lugano in southern Switzerland near the Italian border, where MF and the girls spent about nine months in 1959–60. The girls were enrolled at an academically stringent boarding school, with classes conducted in Italian and French. MF took a room in a house nearby and saw the girls on Wednesdays and Sundays, their only time off. She occupied herself with her work, with learning Italian, and with exploring the town and its environs.

On holiday near Cannes, December 22, 1959. From left, MF, Anna, Kennedy, and Donald and Eleanor Friede.

Christmas, Marseille, 1959. "Insolite. *There seems to be no proper twin for this word in English. . . . Inwardly I know that it means* mysterious, unknowable, *and in plain fact,* indefinable.

"*And that is Marseille: indefinable, and therefore* insolite. *And the strange word is as good as any to explain why the place haunts me and draws me, with its phoenixlike vitality, its implacably realistic beauty and brutality.*"

Anna, Kennedy, and MF in Nice.

In Aix at the Hôtel Roi René, two
days after leaving Lugano, 1960.

The Friedes and the Barrs on
a picnic near L'Harmas, 1960.
Norah and her three boys had
rented a farmhouse not far from
L'Harmas on the other side of Aix.

At L'Harmas, a farm hamlet
about three miles outside Aix on
the Route du Tholonet, where MF
and the girls lived after leaving
Lugano. MF was convinced that
the pure air of her beloved Aix
would quell the persistent cough
that had afflicted her in Swit-
zerland. "Let me get back to Aix, I
prayed. Let me lie in a meadow,
and drink herb teas."

The view from MF's window at the Hôtel de Provence, Aix, where she and the girls moved after leaving L'Harmas. "What I wrote in the quiet room above the rooftops of the old town came out as [A Cordiall Water.]" She dedicated the book to Eleanor Friede.

In Marseille with Anna, Kennedy, the writer Eda Lord, MF's friend from boarding school days, and an affable Marseillais.

On the Ile de Porquerolles off the southeast coast of France, November 1960.

California, ca. 1962. "There are some relationships which send out myriad gangli [sic], into the furthermost tissues of another's soul. When the person dies, these die too. And they must be dug out, dead tissue, by the tiny needles and the surgical tools of strong-willed might. They must be uprooted. But they leave, if handled wisely and removed only for salutary reasons, a beneficent secondary growth, a kind of wisdom. I know this to be true. I can feel the new tissue growing in my attention to the death of NKN [cousin Nan Kennedy Newton]. It was probably the strongest thing in my life since Dillwyn died. Since then David has suicided, and my two parents have died, and and and. But this was the nearest since D. And it seemed to pare away from my hardened soul the callous [sic] of self-protection that I had built, and leave me clean."

In St. Helena, the beginnings of
Map of Another Town.

With Norah in the kitchen on
Oak Avenue, St. Helena, ca. 1963.

Genoa, Nevada, at the foot of the
Sierra, where MF spent the winter
of 1964 continuing work on Map
of Another Town.

With her sister Anne at Anne's home in Genoa, 1964.

In St. Helena, ca. 1964, with Francis "Paco" Gould and Romilda Gould, who with MF were among the seven or eight founding mem- *bers of the Napa Valley Wine Association. Of the Goulds she wrote, "our friendship grew into a fine, lasting thing."*

Ca. 1964, in front of the St. Helena Public Library, which housed the Napa Valley Wine Library. Formed in 1961 as an adjunct to the Wine Association, *the library housed books about wine lore and the rich history of wine making in the Valley and beyond. MF chaired its book selection committee.*

MF with her first grandchild,
Anna's son Chris. Summer,
St. Helena, 1965.

Malibu, ca. 1966. "I am not at all frightened about being old. There are many things I do not like about the actual process of aging, both physical and mental...boring, unpleasant. But they do not scare me. They only bore and displease me.

"There is only one way to avoid most of them, and that is to die first, which I may or may not do. If I live into old age I shall try very hard to make it interesting for myself and not too onerous for the people around me.

"Meanwhile I do not like to head for it with such meaningless speed as seems to be the case here in St. Helena. It is like shooting helplessly down a swift silent river. I want to catch onto a few overhanging branches, not to save myself but simply to feel them in my hands...."

With Barbara Ware, a Piney Woods student MF invited to Oak Avenue with the hope of getting the young woman out of Mississippi and into a nursing career. The experiment, which lasted several months, was trying for them both and only partially successful.

*In St. Helena, with good friend
Marietta Voorhees, ca. 1967.*

*A Time-Life publicity shot with
Michael Field, MF's collaborator
on* The Cooking of Provincial
France. *The work itself was not
entirely rewarding to MF—the
Time-Life editorial process was
frustrating to a writer accustomed
to minimal editorial interfer-
ence—but she was enriched by
the personal and professional
relationships it spawned, most
notably with Julia and Paul
Child, who remained her lifelong
friends.*

*Francis "Paco" Gould's eighty-
eighth birthday celebration, St.
Helena, 1972. From left, Yolande
Beard, MF, Paco Gould, James
Beard. The printer James E. Beard
and his wife Yolande were both
longtime friends and Wine Library
associates of MF's.*

Before leaving the house on Oak Avenue, spring 1970.

In Any Welcoming Life

1970 — 1992

If there is something that pleases and satisfies, it will fall into place in any welcoming life," Fisher wrote, prefacing her appreciation of vegetables, in fact, but the conviction could as well be applied to the two-room *palazzino* she called Last House. The offer to build on David Pleydell-Bouverie's Glen Ellen ranch was fortuitously timed and right in every way. Mary Frances had visited the ranch often as Bouverie's guest and was familiar with the compound that included his home and other dwellings for guests and ranch help. Though he was often gone, Bouverie had a staff in place to look after the ranch in his absence; Mary Frances had the welcome assurance that help was never far away should she need it. Together they conceived a plan for her house, and she made plans to go to France while it was being built. She left with Norah in the fall of 1970 for a trip of several months. They spent time in Aix and visited the Childs in Plascassier before Mary Frances went on alone to Arles and Avignon. Returning to Oak Avenue after Christmas, she began to sort through the years' accumulation, packing up what seemed essential and readying herself spiritually and physically for the move to neighboring Sonoma Valley.

It was not easy to leave St. Helena: "Almost half of my heart was there, sharing honors with Aix-en-Provence." But Mary Frances was entering the last phase of her life and wanted to disengage herself from situations that might compromise her future independence. Last House was designed to accommodate her aging, with simplified space indoors and an expansive view of the Sonoma Valley outdoors. She delighted in it. "It is very simple: I am here because I choose to be," she wrote. Her contentment is echoed in a letter to a friend written in October 1971, several months after she had moved to Glen Ellen: "This place does give me an increasing sense of serenity and, perhaps you are right, joy. I feel very fortunate to know that I am *here* at last. All the other houses in my life were a preparation for this, and I begin to realize how much I learned from them about *now*."

Mary Frances was not yet home to stay. She continued to travel, and accompanied by Norah made three more trips to France in the seventies. *A Considerable Town*, an exploration of her mysterious attachment to Marseille, was written after her last visit there in 1978. They also went to Japan that year at the invitation of the eminent culinary teacher Shizuo Tsuji, spending two weeks at his culinary institute in Osaka, receiving a nearly royal introduction to the art of Japanese cuisine. In return, Mary Frances would write the introduction to Tsuji's book, *Japanese Cooking: A Simple Art*.

As the 1980s approached and with them increasing infirmity, Mary Frances knew she could no longer travel; but she was a great one for taking trips in her mind. "My friend said that 'at eighty, the last thing you feel like doing is planning a journey.'" She insisted on "a complete refutation of that heinous conclusion," and went on to describe the "several journeys a day, and even more than that at night" which she took from bed or bath. The distances were often great—Mexico, Marseille, Athens—but not always; some travels took her no farther than her view. "My eyes keep going out the window to watch the sun on the dancing leaves. My poor old body is out there too. The grass looks beautiful, a sudden tender green after last night's little rain, and the red lava stones look redder than usual, and

the vines have a new fuzz of green on them. In other words I feel like spring."

Although her friend and agent Henry Volkening had died in 1972, Mary Frances was secure in her new relationship with the agent Robert Lescher, to whom she entrusted her literary estate. She continued writing for magazines and over the next ten years would see to the collection of much of her previous work, notably in *As They Were* (1982), *Two Towns in Provence* (1983), *Dubious Honors* (1988), and *Long Ago in France* (1991). Between 1981 and 1989, North Point Press reprinted ten of her books, including *The Art of Eating* series in separate volumes; several fine presses issued editions of short works.

In 1983, Mary Frances published *Sister Age*, a collection of "old age" pieces written from the mid sixties through the early eighties. She had conceived the idea for a book on aging some fifty years previous, when she was curiously inspired by a small portrait of an old woman she found in a Zurich junk shop. From then on she collected notes and older peoples' stories with a book in mind. Although the collection of stories that make up *Sister Age* was not the book she once envisioned, it represented her conviction that "our dispassionate acceptance of attrition be matched by a full use of everything that has ever happened in all the long wonderful-ghastly years to free a person's mind from his body... to use the experience, both great and evil, so that physical annoyances are surmountable in an alert and even mirthful appreciation of life itself."

Despite limits on her mobility and energies, Mary Frances kept the doors of Last House open to visitors. Her renown as a writer and as an equally remarkable woman showed no signs of diminishing: she would be honored by Les Dames d'Escoffier in 1978, receive the prestigious Robert Kirsch Award of the *Los Angeles Times* in 1983, and be elected to the American Academy and Institute of Arts and Letters in 1991.

Mary Frances had weathered periodic spells of creative inactivity throughout her career. She was less prepared to be creatively active yet physically unable to get words down on paper. When complications from Parkinson's disease coupled with poor eyesight threatened to stop her from writing altogether, she fought back with characteristic determination. She experimented with tape recorders and hired assistants to take dictation and type for her, and in the spirit of her armchair travels, she took to writing books in her head, a talent she had cultivated since childhood. (In its advanced stage, the Parkinson's would affect her voice, too, reducing it to a near whisper, and she struggled to conserve it. "I find it increasingly difficult," she wrote when unable to talk on the phone with Robert Lescher, "to be so filled with words and to be so unable to express them.") Mary Frances did not pretend to be unbothered by her ailments and her increased dependence on others, but she coached herself to maintain a philosophical detachment in the face of her own aging; this, being one of the cumulative lessons of a life well lived, allowed her graceful exit. She died of complications from Parkinson's disease on June 22, 1992.

MF, 1974.

*With "Squire" David Pleydell-
Bouverie on the ranch, ca. 1975.*

Last House. "The air is mostly dry and sweet, where I have chosen to stay. During the rains it is soft with seasonal perfumes of meadow grasses and new leaves. By mid-April the cows are back from their winter pasturage, usually heavy with imminent calvings, and they tread down myriad wild flowers into the volcanic ash that makes up much of this valley's earth. . . .

I find this house a never-ending excitement, and I think that this is as necessary when a person is in the seventies as in the teens and twenties. What is more, knowing why and where is much easier and more fun in one's later years, even if such enjoyment may have to be paid for with a few purely physical hindrances, like crickety fingers or capricious eyesight."

*Inside Last House: the working
order of MF's desk and bookshelves
in a corner of the main room,
which accommodated kitchen,
dining, and work space in the
context of a generous living room.
From its adjoining balcony, MF
looked "due west into a low range
of wooded hills that are a county
park, with easy trails, and then on
to the high blue mountains of the
Jack London Preserve."*

In the kitchen and by the fireplace.

The bathroom at Last House was "large and low, with probably the biggest tub in this region, and a capacious shower and a long counter, all sane and practical but voluptuous. . . . One long wall is painted the same Pompeian red as the ceiling, and has a changing pattern of pictures I feel like looking at for a time."

With Norah in Paris, 1974. "It would be impossible for me ever to recount the ways I have existed in that place. I have told a few. But one thing I can repeat, that when my youngest sister and my brother, she twenty and he eighteen I believe, came there and I met them, while I was living in Switzerland, I said to my husband, 'Oh, I could weep for them—it is not the beautiful place it was when I first came to it in 1929. The quays have changed, trees are down, the taxis all have tops— oh, no!' He looked at me in a remote smiling way and said, 'I once could have wept for you. Nineteen twenty-nine! What a crude year! You did not know Paris when it was Paris, in 1915, when I came back after seventeen days at the front and the janitor of the little Hôtel Foyot above the restaurant cut off my boots and bathed me and after I had slept for twenty hours brought me a bowl of wild strawberries. No, poor you. You never knew—and your brother and sister will pity their youngsters just as you and I...'"

On the porch at Last House, 1977.

"People collect Last Words, hoping to hear the truth.

"I remember sitting in a dim hospital room with my paternal grandmother. I was leaving (from Los Angeles for San Francisco), and her thick snow-white hair had been cut off to make it easier for the nurses. My next-younger sister had just had a child, and Grandmother thought it was ridiculous that the baby could not be brought down from SF to the Murphy Memorial Hospital in Whittier, California, so that she could see him. (This was, in those days, about 525 miles.) She told me, in a nonchalant way, that when one of her four sons, of which my father was one, had been born, she was loaded into a sleigh and packed about with buffalo robes and taken to Peach-Blow Farm, so that her own grandmother could take a look.

"I had nothing to say about this.

"But inside my head was something that still rings there, hums there. I wanted to cry out, GRAND-MOTHER, TELL ME. Tell me what? Why tell me? I never did. But I now feel that perhaps she was waiting for me to ask it, and that perhaps she would have...

"I don't think that I could ask it now. But it is always in my secret rhythm...

"Who wants to know? Everybody, but nobody. I look at the good faces of people older than I, and I see them with my approaching knowledge, people like Paco Gould and Janet Flanner, both so fine and in the wine-sense 'fined'...and do I really need to know more than what their faces are telling me?

"This may be one of the truths of the aging process: a common acceptance, at least among . . . the knowing wise prescient people, . . . of what is happening. . . . In their own ways, they have readied themselves, if they are indeed intelligent."

In Osaka, Japan, with Norah, 1978. "Of course, we were treated like duchesses, only a rung or two below the Imperial family on the caste-ladder," MF wrote of her two-week stay in Osaka. While "watching some forty-five private demonstrations at the two Tsuji buildings in Osaka . . . and coping with about thirty gastronomical onslaughts, no matter how gently subtle, in restaurants and inns and street-shops," MF conducted her instinctual gastro-cultural study: "The preparation and serving of fine as well as routine Japanese food is more obviously mixed, than is ours, with other things than hunger.

"At its best, it is inextricably meshed with aesthetics, with religion, with tradition and history. It is evocative of seasonal changes, or of one's childhood, or of a storm at sea: one thin slice of molded fish puree shaped like a maple leaf and delicately colored orange and scarlet, to celebrate autumn; a tiny hut made of carved ice, with a little fish inside made of chestnut paste and a chestnut made of fish paste, to remind an

honored guest that he was born on a far-north island; an artfully stuffed lobster riding an angry sea of curled waves of white radish cut paper-thin, with occasional small shells of carved shrimp-meat tossing helplessly in the troughs...

"All this delicate pageantry is based on things that we Westerners are either unaware of or that we accept for vaguely sentimental reasons. . . . We have never been taught to make little look like much, make much out of little, in a mystical combination of ascetic and aesthetic as well as animal satisfaction."

*With her friend Judith Clancy
at an exhibit of Clancy's Gare de
Lyon drawings in San Francisco,
1980. The artist's drawings had
been published the previous year
in a book titled* Not a Station
but a Place *with an introduction
by MF.*

Ca. 1985.

With Charlie, 1985.

At Last House, with longtime assistant Marsha Moran, 1985.

In 1985 with a group of North Point Press authors; editor-in-chief Jack Shoemaker and publisher William Turnbull in foreground; Leslie Scalapino, Edward Schafer, MF, and Page Smith in middle row; Evan Connell, Gina Berriault, Lawrence DiStasi, Ronald Johnson, Michael McClure, Bruce Coleman, David Meltzer, Anne Lamott, and Don Carpenter in back row.

MF loved this caricature by the artist David Levine. It appeared in The New York Review of Books, December 7, 1989.

With William Turnbull (left) and Jack Shoemaker.

Visitors to Last House over the years:

With Maya Angelou, ca. 1984.

Chuck Williams, James A. Beard,
Julia Child. January 9, 1977.

With Craig Claiborne, May 1985.

With Bert Greene, ca. 1984.

With a good friend from San Francisco, Henrietta Humphries, ca. 1991.

With Anna, Kennedy, and Anna's children, Matthew and Sylvie, ca. 1989.

"I have tried not to mislead readers, just because I used words better than they did. (I have never told them to add marshmallows to their chicken salad!) In general I think that I have been trusted to state the facts.

"But now I feel tired. I want to stop. But I don't know what will happen when I do, and that puzzles me and perhaps scares me a little.

"I am deteriorating physically at what seems a rather fast rate. Cataracts on both eyes, increasing palsy / tremor on right side (Parkinson's Disease is the casual diagnosis, but I think that may be a modern evasion of the general Aging Process...)...lameness and numb feet, and above all what could be called FATIGUE: these are symptoms of my mortality!

"I do not like them. I feel chained. But increasingly I recognize in others that my desires are growing calmer, and that it does not much matter to me about putting an idea on paper as long as I can take a nap.

"I've called this a form of euthanasia when I've watched it happen. Now it is happening to me, and all I want to do is bow to it. I meant to work longer, and to say more. But if my body has called off the whole thing, I am quiescent."

"So I dawdle. I put off looking at the mail. I get out a recipe, but I wait until later to make it. (I even get out all the ingredients and put the recipe near them, and then I lie on my bed, under my warm soft pouf.)

"This morning I asked myself when in the rest of my unnatural life I had dawdled. Perhaps when I was about fourteen, when I was a miserable human brat. Or perhaps when I was drifting arrogantly from one college to another, I coasted. I slept, or I cleaned all night, or I played tennis. But perhaps I was not dawdling (wasteful human lazy behavior). Perhaps I was waiting.

"I was waiting to escape from being entre deux âges when I was fourteen. Later I was waiting to escape from my young life, which then meant losing my virginity and marrying into another physical and even mental world.

"So now I understand that I am not dawdling. I am waiting. I am waiting to move on, which at my age means dying. I wonder about how best to do it, most neatly. I must now wait, to learn more."

"The priests and the storytellers, the great singers and the teachers, everywhere and always showed their people real food, real wine, to prove to them the truths of spiritual nourishment. A great catch of fishes from an empty sea, or water springing from a dry stone: such things were told of over and over to sustain men whose hope of Heaven dwindled and grew faint as their stomachs cried out."

"*And with our gastronomical growth will come, inevitably, knowledge and perception of a hundred other things, but mainly of ourselves.*"

"*[My first husband] stood by his conviction, that if people know real happiness anywhere, they must never expect to find it there again. . . . Perhaps his stubbornness was admirable, but his refusal to change his idée fixe was plain stupid, to my older wiser mind. Who always wants to look at a café or an altar or an oak tree with the first innocence and the limited understanding of a naive lovesick girl, or a homesick born-again Byron?*

"*Five minutes or five centuries from now, we will see changeless realities with new eyes.*"

"It seems to me now . . . that the only real thing to leave in the world is one's spirit. . . . To me it means that I can leave, for whatever use may be made of it . . . , a kind of residue. I believe that it is good. I hope so. It is the leavings of me, murking up the atmosphere, smogging the air, sprinkling a sort of mist over things so that perhaps they will twinkle a bit."

From George Santayana, a quotation MF used as epigraph to The Gastronomical Me: *"To be happy you must have taken the measure of your powers, tasted the fruits of your passion, and learned your place in the world."*

Bibliography

AG   *An Alphabet for Gourmets*. San Francisco: North Point Press, 1989. Orig. pub. 1949.

AF   *Among Friends*. San Francisco: North Point Press, 1983. Orig. pub. 1970.

——   *The Art of Eating*. New York: Vintage Books, 1976. Orig. pub. 1954.

ATW   *As They Were*. New York: Vintage Books, 1983.

——   *The Boss Dog*. San Francisco: North Point Press, 1991.

——   *Consider the Oyster*. San Francisco: North Point Press, 1988. Orig. pub. 1941.

CT   *A Considerable Town* from *Two Towns in Provence*. New York: Vintage Books, 1983. Orig. pub. 1964.

CF   *Conversations with M. F. K. Fisher* (David Lazar, ed.). Jackson, Mississippi: University Press of Mississippi, 1992.

——   *The Cooking of Provincial France* (Julia Child and Michael Field, consulting eds.). New York: Time-Life Books, 1968.

CW   *A Cordiall Water: A Garland of Odd and Old Receipts to Assuage the Ills of Man and Beast*. San Francisco: North Point Press, 1981. Orig. pub. 1961.

DH   *Dubious Honors*. San Francisco: North Point Press, 1988.

GM   *The Gastronomical Me*. San Francisco: North Point Press, 1989. Orig. pub. 1943.

HLF   *Here Let Us Feast: A Book of Banquets*. San Francisco: North Point Press, 1986. Orig. pub. 1946.

HCW   *How to Cook a Wolf*. San Francisco: North Point Press, 1988. Orig. pub. 1942.

LH   *Last House: Reflections, Dreams, and Observations 1943–1991*. New York: Pantheon Books, 1995.

LAF   *Long Ago in France*. New York: Touchstone, 1992. Orig. pub. 1991.

MAT   *Map of Another Town: A Memoir of Provence* from *Two Towns in Provence*. New York: Vintage Books, 1983. Orig. pub. 1964.

NN   *Not Now but* Now. San Francisco: North Point Press, 1982. Orig. pub. 1947.

——   Jean Anthelme Brillat-Savarin, *The Physiology of Taste, or Meditations on Transcendental Gastronomy* (translated and annotated by MFK Fisher). Washington, D. C.: Counterpoint, 1995. San Francisco: North Point Press, 1986. Orig. pub. 1949.

SIF   *Serve It Forth*. San Francisco: North Point Press, 1989. Orig. pub. 1937.

SA   *Sister Age*. New York: Vintage Books, 1984. Orig. pub. 1983.

SM   *Stay Me, Oh Comfort Me: Journals and Stories 1933–1941*. New York and San Francisco: Pantheon Books, 1993.

——   *The Story of Wine in California*. Berkeley: University of California Press, 1962.

TBA   *To Begin Again: Stories and Memoirs 1908–1929*. New York and San Francisco: Pantheon Books, 1992.

WBK   *With Bold Knife and Fork*. New York: G. P. Putnam's Sons, 1968, 1969.

Source Citations

Listing by page number. Abbreviations for works cited are found in the Bibliography.

1   "sprang full-blown": TBA, 14.

"a shy, proud": TBA, 9.

"Rex decided": TBA, 9.

"Grandmother did not believe": TBA, 53–54.

2   "She flowed": AF, 64.

"completely happy": TBA, 13.

"two years of": a profile written for Dr. George Frumkes, January 12, 1950.

"And as soon as I could": TBA, 178.

"in a supreme effort": AF, 21.

4   "a strange combination": AF, 226.

"the gawky young journalist": AF, 24.

"Part of his nature": AF, 45.

5   "Rex was in love": AF, 47–48.

"A fine place, indeed": TBA, 13.

   "several plausible causes": AF, 279–80.

6   "My Father often spoke": AF, 282–83.

"I still feel embarrassed": TBA, 14.

7   "small stout autocrat": TBA, 58–59.

"One of the best": AF, 260.

"The two refugees": AF, 261.

"the faintest excuse": AF, 265.

8   "a giant": AF, 5.

"possessing great strength": SA, 4.

"and even Anglo-American": AF, 5.

"constitutionally opposed": TBA, 134, 136–37.

9   "As I see it now": AF, 121–22.

10   "Age is enormous": AF, 170.

11   "Related by love": AF, 62.

"More and more Mother handed": AF, 67.

"All I could now say": AF, 81.

"fine together": AF, 95.

12   "always a pleasurable invasion": AF, 75.

"Edith was probably": AF, 229.

13 "Rex wanted a son": AF, 59.

"beautiful orchard and citrus": AF, 247.

14 "I am the first to admit": AF, 291.

"When I was fifteen": DH, 132.

15 "One time when he looked": TBA, 168.

17 "In 1929": GM, 40.

"It was there": LAF, xiv.

"a man destined": profile written for Dr. George
Frumkes, January 12, 1950.

18 "by the end of the long teatime": DH, 134.

"I was so involved": profile for Dr. Frumkes.

"I was a woman condemned": GM, 209.

19 "consumed by a desire": profile for Dr. Frumkes.

20 "There I was": LAF, xiv.

21 "the biggest, as well": LAF, 31, 34.

22 "Dijon was really not": LAF, 25.

"a fine relationship": LAF, 110.

24 "One time Al": LAF, 40–41.

25 "César was all": SIF, 141.

"The next time we put": GM, 118.

26 "I was already beginning": GM, 101.

29 "Un pâquis": GM, 149–50.

30 "A worker digging": a caption in Fisher's hand on the back
of the photograph.

"The walls are going up": SM, 95.

31 "The only review": unpublished journal, January 7, 1950.

"Flagons and apples": SM, 109.

32 "The part of the house": GM, 154.

33 "[Tim] was a fine gardener": GM, 151–52.

34 "This period was embarrassing": profile for Dr. Frumkes.

35 "My whole existence": SM, 136.

36 "I notice two things": SM, 158–59.

37 "painted like a possessed devil": profile for Dr. Frumkes.

39 "Our land was bare": SM, 339–40.

40 "We stayed aloof": SM, 344–48.

41 "After Tim died": SM, 347–48.

43 "frightful grief": SM, 323.

"I must stop": SM, 323.

"I did it in a few days": DH, 135–36.

44 "the sterile creative life": cited on page 49 by Joan
Reardon, M. F. K. Fisher, Julia Child, and Alice Waters.
New York: Harmony Books, 1994.

"without Tim's cold judicial ear": unpublished letter to
Lawrence Powell, (early) 1943.

"a very personal book": DH, 136.

"a dynamic and restless person": DH, 137.

"The whole long summer": DH, 138.

46 "I try to live": SM, 322.

47 "One morning we were sitting": GM, 226–28.

48 "I remember that I wrote": DH, 135.

"it seemed quite natural": DH, 136.

49 "to my sister Anne": DH, 136.

"The prettifiers of human passion": AG, 135.

50 "Anne is right": unpublished letter to Lawrence Powell,
November 3, 1943.

52 "As for dining-in-love": AG, 54.

53 "We had a summer lease": DH, 138.

54 "Pascal Covici": afterword to NN.

"For some thirty-eight years": LH, 237–40.

56 "We are in debt" and "wavering values": unpublished
journal, December 4, 1946.

57 "I have always felt": unpublished journal, January 11, 1947.

58 "we understood each other": CF, 140.

59 "I am keeping a Line-a-Day book": unpublished journal,
July 26, 1947.

60 "a kind of horrified excitement": unpublished journal,
July 29, 1947.

61 "I've always been pleased": DH, 140.

62 "It is two years ago now": unpublished journal, July 31, 1949.

63 "I see the children": unpublished journal, July 31, 1949.

"Well, I see now": unpublished journal, June 8, 1950.

65 "I seem to go": unpublished letter [to Michel LeGouis?], January 2, 1957.

66 "By letting my girls see": unpublished letter to Fisher's uncle, Ted Kennedy, December 8, 1958.

"This old lady": MAT, 71.

"brutal rude": ATW, 113.

"it was not at all right": unpublished letter [to Michel LeGouis?], January 2, 1957.

"Life was really fine": DH, 141.

"we seemed to have": MAT, 110.

"The second time we left Aix": MAT, 241.

67 "I am preoccupied": unpublished letter to Thomas B. Congdon Jr., July 21, 1964.

68 "a hurried but well-documented survey": unpublished letter to Judith Jones, November 20, 1966.

"a kind of pied-à-terre": ATW, 241. (Originally appeared as the introduction to Not a Station But a Place by Judith S. Clancy, Synergistic Press, 1979.)

69 "I sweated like a stevedore": DH, 144.

"to go back to my own cave": unpublished letter to Grace Holmes, February 4, 1970.

"especially since he proposed": ATW, 259.

70 "I had decided to move": LH, 205.

71 "one of the dearest friends": DH, 140.

72 "I find myself going back": unpublished journal, May 16, 1952.

73 "After Rex died": DH, 140–41.

74 "I knew, the first time": from "Napa and Sonoma: The Best of Both Worlds," The International Review of Wine and Food, August 1979.

75 "A part of me would withdraw": SA, 30.

"The main street": unpublished letter to MF's uncle, Ted Kennedy, June 25, 1954.

76 "We have three little bedrooms": unpublished letter to Ted Kennedy, Easter 1955.

"I meant to put the children": unpublished letter to June Eddy, May 12, 1955.

77 "Things being as they are": unpublished letter to Ted Kennedy, January 26, 1955.

"That was where Cézanne had lived": ATW, 114.

78 "I was feeling disturbed": unpublished letter to Ted Kennedy, July 29, 1955.

79 "People grew used to the fact": LH, 107.

80 "Part of the space": LH, 105.

82 "Insolite": CT, 5.

83 "Let me get back to Aix": MAT, 110.

84 "What I wrote in the quiet room": preface to CW.

85 "There are some relationships": unpublished journal, St. Helena, November 1962.

87 "our friendship grew": tribute to Francis Gould, February 8, 1991.

88 "I am not at all frightened": unpublished letter to Marietta Voorhees, October 1963.

91 "If there is something that pleases": WBK, 162.

"Almost half of my heart was there": ATW, 258.

"It is very simple": ATW, 251.

92 "This place does give me": unpublished letter to Moggs [?] October 18, 1971.

"My friend said": LH, 234.

"My eyes keep going": LH, 277.

"our dispassionate acceptance": SA, 237.

93 "I find it increasingly difficult": unpublished letter to Robert Lescher, April 5, 1989.

94 "The air is mostly dry and sweet": ATW, 259–60.

95 "due west into a low range": ATW, 257.

96　"large and low": ATW, 256–57.

　　"It would be impossible": LH, 53.

97　"People collect Last Words": unpublished journal, January
　　1, 1972.

98　"Of course, we were treated": DH, 50–54.

104　"I have tried not to mislead": unpublished journal, March
　　29, 1981.

105　"So I *dawdle*": LH, 191–92.

106　"The priests and the storytellers": HLF, 7.

107　"And with our gastronomical growth": HCW, 200.

108　"[My first husband] stood by his conviction": LH, 178, 183.

109　"It seems to me now": unpublished journal, January 19,
　　1972.

Photographic Credits

The vast majority of the pictures in this book come from a collection Mary Frances Kennedy Fisher amassed throughout her life. Exceptions and photographers' credits are listed below. Every reasonable effort has been made to clear the use of photographs in this volume with copyright owners.

13   Kennedy Friede Golden revisited her picture collection countless times and provided this photograph, among others, of her mother with siblings, and Grandmother Holbrook.

14   Mary Frances with David, Norah, and Anne, courtesy of Kennedy Friede Golden.

19   The wedding portrait of Mary Frances was taken by the acclaimed Hollywood portraitist George Hurrell, who photographed her on many occasions over many years.

20   Map of Dijon copyright © Claudia Carlson, 1990.

21   The illustration of Chef Racouchot (drawn by Georges Conrad, 1930, Paris) was provided by Jean-François Bazin, president of the Conseil Regional de Bourgogne, and an admirer of Fisher's.

     The photographs of the rooftops and streets of Dijon are the property of the city photographic archives housed at the Bibliothèque Municipale, Dijon.

22   The photograph of Lawrence Powell and Mary Frances on the street in Dijon belonged to Powell, who gave it to Norah Kennedy Barr. It is reproduced here with her permission.

27   The portrait of Gigi and Dillwyn Parrish by the photographer William Mortensen was kindly provided by Mrs. John Weld, formerly Gigi Parrish.

31   Faith Echtermeyer in St. Helena, California, photographed the copies of *Serve It Forth*, as well as the other first edition titles that appear on pages 48, 49, and 61.

35   Mary Frances with Dillwyn Parrish at the Ritz Hotel, Paris, courtesy of Kennedy Friede Golden.

39   The three photographs of Bareacres from Fisher's collection were taken in 1946 by Man Ray.

46   Copyright © George Hurrell, 1942.

48   Publicity photographs copyright © John Engstead, 1942.

49   (top right) Copyright © John Engstead, ca. 1944.

51   The globe was photographed for this book by Faith Echtermeyer.

52   Donald Friede, photographed by Man Ray, 1946.

54   Pascal Covici Jr. kindly contributed the photograph of his father.

The photograph of Henry Volkening with Diarmuid Russell is reprinted courtesy of Eudora Welty.

58   Man Ray took the photographs of Mary Frances and Kennedy on the patio at Bareacres in October 1946.

62   Photographs by Man Ray, 1946.

77   *Mont Sainte-Victoire* by Paul Cézanne courtesy of the Philadelphia Museum of Art: George W. Elkins Collection.

87   The photograph of Mary Frances in front of the St. Helena Public Library is reprinted courtesy of the Napa Valley Wine Library.

89   The photograph of Mary Frances and Michael Field is from *Foods of the World: Provincial France*, copyright © 1968 Time-Life Books, Inc. All rights reserved.

93   Mary Frances, photographed by her nephew, Matthew Barr, 1974.

95   Mary Frances in the kitchen and by the fireplace, copyright © Paul Harris.

96   At top right is one of a series of photographs taken by George Hurrell on a visit to Last House in 1984, just a few months before he died. At this reunion after more than thirty years, he is reported to have said, "God damn, Mary Frances, nobody knows your bones but me!" Portrait courtesy of Kennedy Friede Golden.

97   Photograph by Paul Child, 1977. Mary Frances greatly admired Child's photographs, especially those he shot in Provence. On more than one occasion, she proposed their collaboration on a book of his Provençal photographs, for which she would provide the text.

99   Mary Frances and Judith Clancy, January 1, 1980, photographed by and courtesy of Bud Johns.

99–100   The portrait of Mary Frances and the photograph with Charlie were taken at the 1984 session with George Hurrell.

100   Mary Frances with Marsha Moran, copyright © and courtesy of Art Rogers/Pt. Reyes.

101   Photographs from a North Point Press session, copyright © Thomas Victor, 1985.

Drawing by David Levine. Reprinted with permission from *The New York Review of Books*, copyright © 1989 Nyrev, Inc.

102   Chuck Williams, James A. Beard, and Julia Child photographed by Paul Child, January 9, 1977.

Mary Frances and Maya Angelou, copyright © Paul Fusco/Magnum Photo.

103   Mary Frances and Bert Greene, copyright © Paul Fusco/Magnum Photo.

104   Copyright © Paul Fusco/Magnum Photo.

105   Copyright © Margaret Fabrizio.

106   (upper left) Copyright © Paul Fusco/Magnum Photo; (upper right) copyright © Janet Fries; (bottom) copyright © Paul Fusco/Magnum Photo.

107   (top) Copyright © and courtesy of Bill Bridges. (bottom) copyright © Paul Harris.

108   (upper left) Copyright © and courtesy of Roger Mueller; (lower left) copyright © and courtesy of Richard Foorman; (right) copyright © Parente.

109   Copyright © Joanie Morgan. Andrews Hall, Sonoma, California, March 19, 1989.

Acknowledgments

Many people have helped me in assembling this book, but my first thanks are to Jack Shoemaker, editor-in-chief at Counterpoint, and to Robert Lescher, M. F. K. Fisher's agent and literary executor, both for giving me the chance to undertake the project and for standing so firmly behind me once I did.

To all those whose help I enlisted in my search for additional photographs, I add sweeping thanks to the mention of their names in the photographic credits.

My thanks go as well to Kennedy Friede Golden, who was unfailingly generous with her time, her support, and her memories of her mother.

— to Norah Kennedy Barr for her help in identifying photographs from her sister's childhood and young adulthood, and for correcting inaccuracies in my text.

— to Marsha and Pat Moran for helpful access to their office and the Fisher files under their guardianship.

— to my friend Amy Wilner, who reviewed the manuscript and provided encouragement.

— to Carole McCurdy, managing editor at Counterpoint, for her tireless work in seeing the book through production, and to David Bullen for its beautiful design.

Finally, I am indebted to Ross Feld for his help as editor and friend, and to my husband, whose support has many guises, large and small.

This book is dedicated to the memory of my father, D. Frederick Gioia.

9/16/97

B   Fisher, M. F. K.
Fisher   (Mary Frances
           Kennedy), 1908-

           A welcoming life.

$35.00